LOST YORK COUNTY

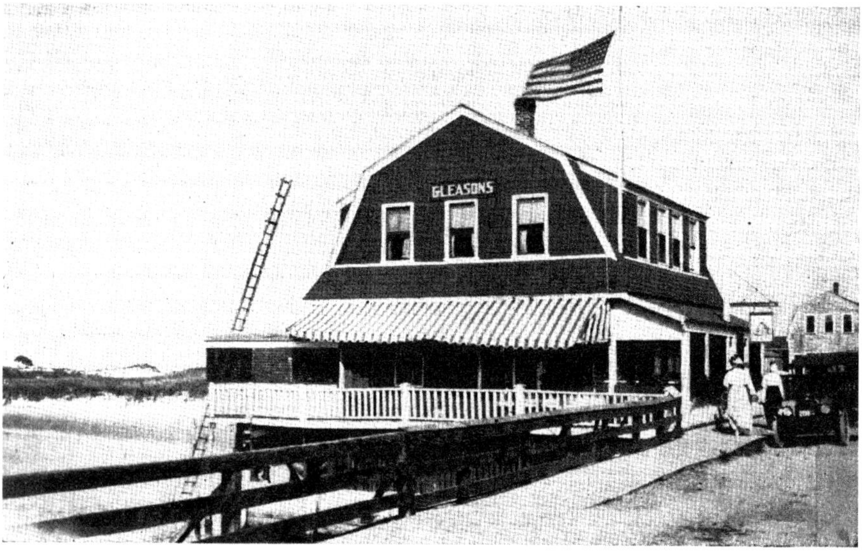

Gleason's Lobster House in Ogunquit served customers hot lobsters and was in business around 1918. A period ad placed the business on Beach Road.

LOST YORK COUNTY

STEVEN BURR

THE History PRESS

Published by The History Press
Charleston, SC 29403
www.historypress.net

All images are courtesy of the author unless otherwise noted.

First published 2009

Manufactured in the United States

ISBN 978.1.59629.551.3

Library of Congress Cataloging-in-Publication Data

Burr, Steven.
Lost landmarks of York County / Steven A. Burr.
p. cm.
Includes bibliographical references.
ISBN 978-1-59629-551-3
1. York County (Me.)--History, Local. 2. York County (Me.)--History, Local--Pictorial works. 3. Historic buildings--Maine--York County. 4. Historic buildings--Maine--York County--Pictorial works. I. Title.
F27.Y6B87 2008
974.1'9504--dc22
2008055284

This book is dedicated to my grandchildren:
Amber Skye Bryant, Baby Hutton and Jaymee Merrick.

Contents

Acknowledgements

I have many people to thank for helping me complete this book. I really appreciate the time and generosity of all those who shared their photographs and research for this project. As always, thanks to Greg Hubbard, for editing and letting me ramble and for the use of his photographs; a special thanks to Ruth Bridges Ayer for sharing her research; also Harland Eastman and the Sanford-Springvale Historical Society; Joyce Butler; Brian Cincotta, for generously sharing his photographs; Linda Aaskov and Elizabeth Morrison, Friends of the Alfred Shakers Museum; Wendy Persig and Norma Keim, the Old Berwick Historical Society; Limington Historical Society; Jane Edgecomb, the Wells-Ogunquit Historical Society; the Parsonsfield-Porter Historical Society; the Newfield Historical Society; Rosanne Adams, Eliot Baha'i Archives; Rosalind Magnuson, Brick Store Museum; Judith Buckman, town clerk, Berwick; Don Sheldon; and the staff and volunteers at the following libraries: Dyer Library, Saco; Rice Library, Kittery; Berwick Library; Kennebunk Free Library; Wells Public Library; Fog Library, Eliot; Hurd Library, North Berwick; McArthur Library, Biddeford; Parsons Library, Alfred. Hopefully I have not forgotten anyone—if I have, my apologies.

Introduction

Located in the southwestern corner of the state, York County is Maine's front door. Travelers arriving from the south enter Maine through one of the county's oldest towns, Kittery, repeating the journey made by French, British and Spanish settlers centuries ago. Forests of first-growth white pine drew many of these settlers, especially Scots, and spurred the construction of sawmills and small towns along York County's many rivers and streams. White pines grew straight and tall and made sturdy masts sought by England's shipping industry. They were also sawn into lumber that was exported to England and other countries. York, Kittery, Wells, Kennebunk, Kennebunkport, Saco and Biddeford grew into centers of shipbuilding and shipping, while inland towns formed around farms and mills.

Confronted with such a rich history, choosing images for this book proved challenging. I have tried to avoid famous lost landmarks, those that have appeared in books and magazines and are well known by the public. Instead, I have sought lesser-known—but equally important—landmarks that have disappeared and been forgotten. Locating images proved difficult as well. While York County's coastal towns appear in many postcards and other period images, photographs of inland towns are rare.

Additionally, I have tried to broaden the concept of a landmark by including seemingly ordinary buildings that have played a role in everyday affairs. I hope this will help us remember that a wide range of structures act as landmarks. For example, in addition to those associated with major events or individuals, we mention certain buildings, often an old business or home, when giving directions. Too often, we drive by these buildings without paying attention, until one day we pass by and realize they are gone.

CHAPTER ONE

HOMES OF YORK COUNTY, MAINE

Many private homes in York County have been lost over the years. It would take an entire book, larger than this one, just to record them. A few of the homes in this chapter still stand but were included because they have been significantly altered or fallen into disrepair.

Development projects claimed some of these homes. Urban renewal projects in Sanford, for example, destroyed dozens of buildings that might otherwise have been restored. Similarly, important landmarks along Route 1, between Kittery and Scarborough, have been replaced by commercial development. In other instances, buildings were destroyed for retail projects that were never completed, leaving behind vacant lots and robbing towns of their history.

Fire has destroyed many more of York County's landmarks. The fire of 1947, which burned over 200,000 acres of land, leveled nine communities and caused an estimated $30 million in losses. The blaze began in Newfield on October 17, decimating the town before moving toward the coast. Kennebunk narrowly escaped, but nearby Goose Rocks Beach was leveled and only six buildings survived in Fortune's Rock. The fire reached Cape Porpoise before a change in the wind direction saved most of that town and Kennebunkport.

In addition to the challenges of development and fire, preservationists have struggled to convince people of the need to preserve local landmarks. Buildings perish one at a time, which can make the loss seem insignificant. As the number of lost landmarks grows, entire downtown and residential districts disappear. Many cities and towns across the United States have become aware of this problem and have enacted laws to protect what remains. Unfortunately, York County has not learned that lesson, and the destruction of local landmarks continues.

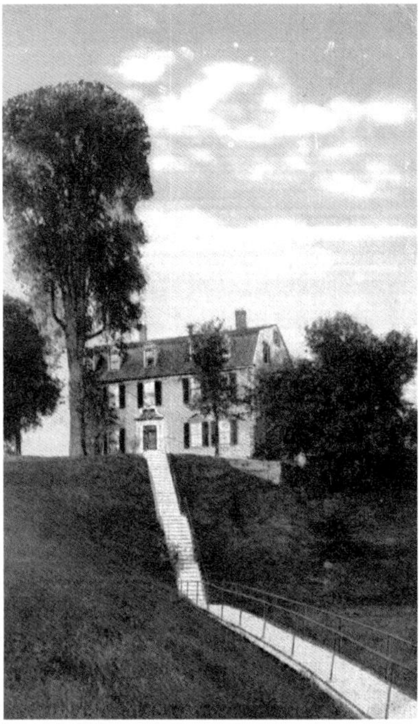

This late Georgian home was completed for Colonel Thomas Cutts in 1782 and stood on York Hill (Factory Island) in Saco. Cutts owned and operated several mills across from his home. In 1937, Central Maine Power bought the property for a substation. Many accounts falsely report that the home was saved. However, the first floor, which contained the principal rooms with detailed paneling and woodwork, was demolished and the top two floors were moved to Glen Haven Circle in Saco.

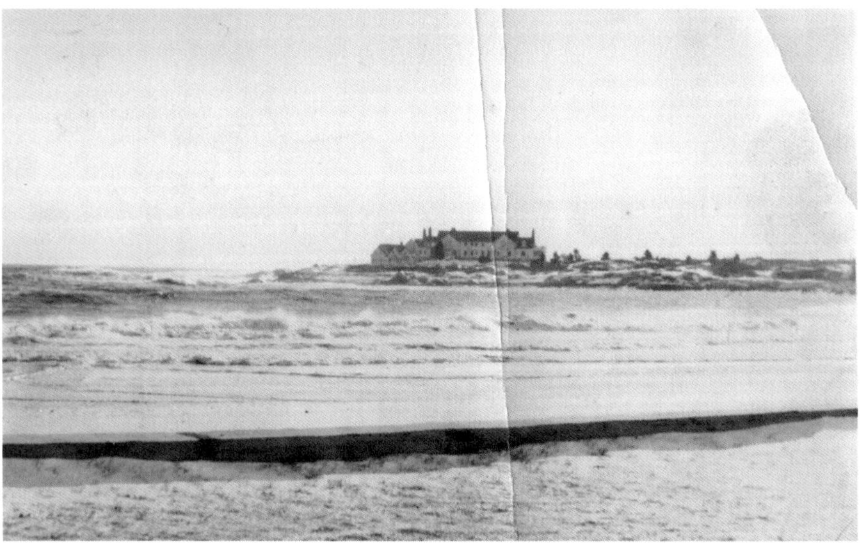

Crawford W. Livingston had this summer cottage built at Granite Point, Biddeford, in 1913. It was one of the largest "cottages" built at Granite Point and had twenty rooms, six bathrooms and a ballroom. It burned on February 17, 1965, while being demolished. Livingston was a stockbroker, banker and railroad builder who was from St. Paul, Minnesota. The town of Livingston, Montana, was named for him. *Courtesy of McArthur Library.*

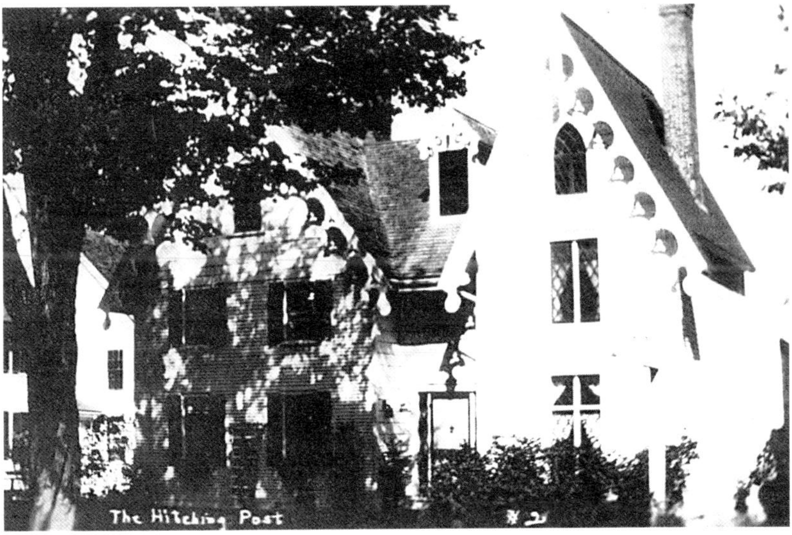

Felicia Cleaves acquired this Kennebunkport home from her father in 1876 and transformed the home with Gothic details. After the remodeling, her neighbors began referring to the home as "Aunt Felicia's Folly." New owners in 1966 restored the home to how it may have looked when it was first built in the early 1800s. It still stands, but it was a shame to lose the Gothic details that made the home unique. *Courtesy of Greg Hubbard.*

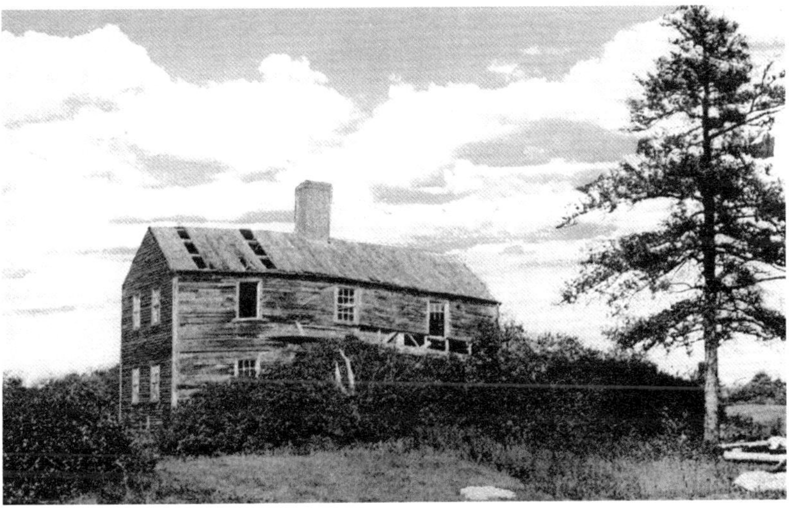

This circa 1935 postcard shows the eighteenth-century Durrell home, which stood on Durrell's Bridge Road in Kennebunk. It was located on the left, after the bridge, on the Arundel side beside the Kennebunk River. The Durrell family were early settlers to the Kennebunks and suffered great hardships trying to establish themselves there. They were attacked by Indians several times, and some of the family members were taken to Canada, where they managed to escape.

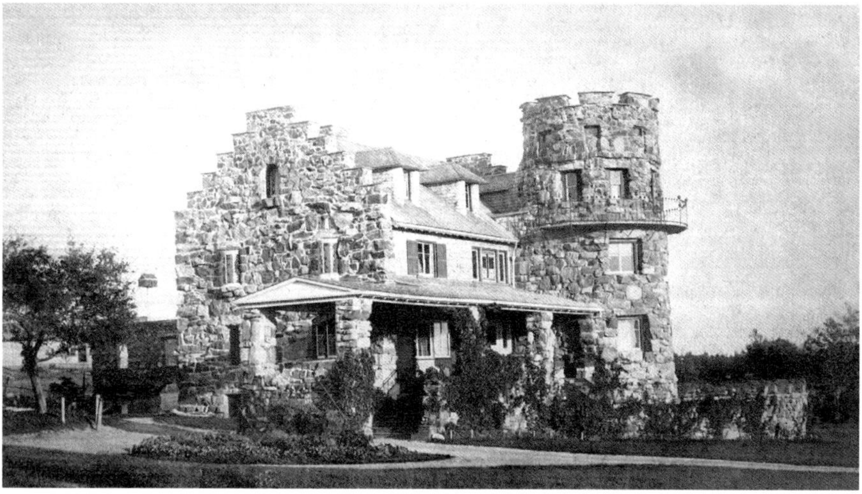

This Kennebunkport summer home was owned by the Clark family, who built it after their first cottage burned. The stones for the three-foot-thick walls were collected from along the nearby beaches. Unfortunately, those stones made the home damp and over time salt began to leach out from them, making the home unlivable. Locals dubbed the cottage "the Castle" for its turret and rock walls. It was demolished in 1911. *Courtesy of Greg Hubbard.*

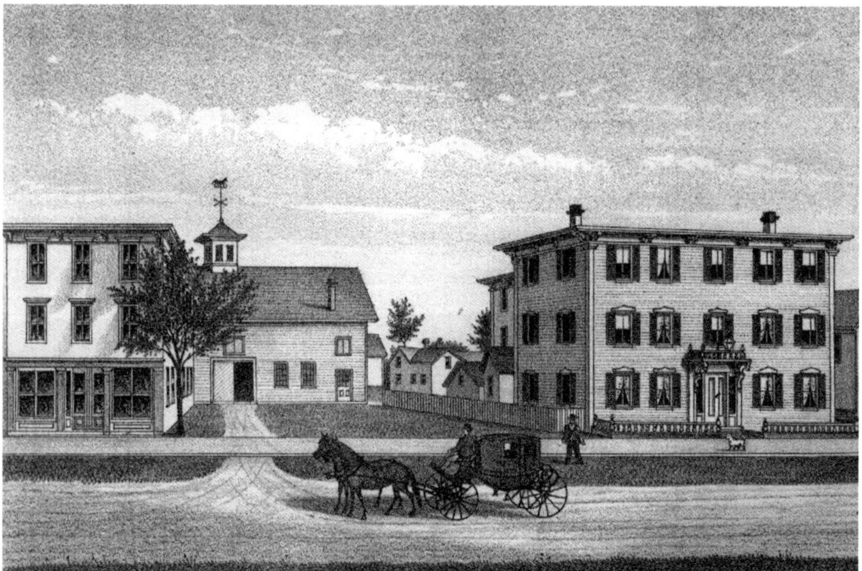

Samuel Nasson purchased this Sanford home, on the right, in 1845 and opened it as an inn called the Mousam River House. In 1870, George Nasson, Samuel's son, closed the hotel but continued to live there. After his death, the home was reopened as a hotel but was demolished in 1972 under Sanford's Urban Renewal Program. *From* History of York County.

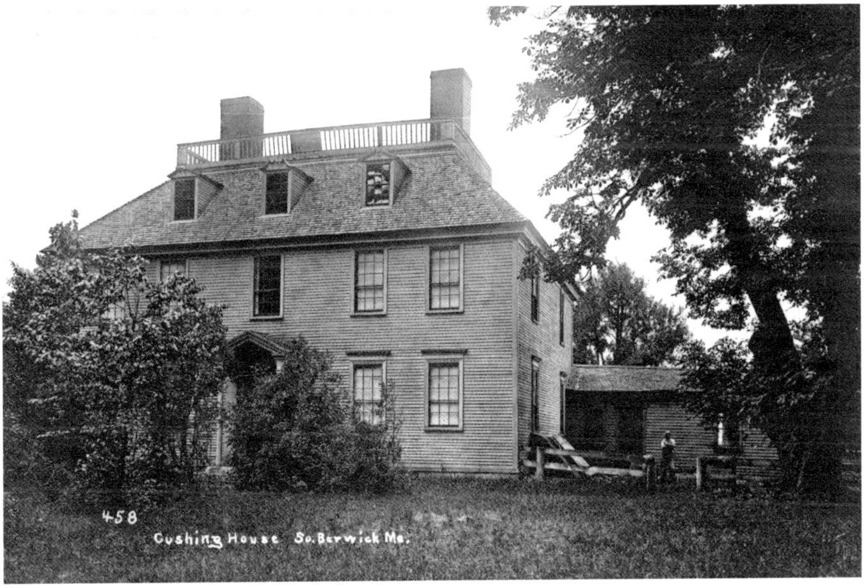

The Cushing mansion, built in 1795, stood on Main Street in South Berwick. Elizabeth Wallingford had the house built for her daughter and son-in-law, Olive and John Cushing, on the condition that they move back to South Berwick and allow her to live with them. During the Revolution, the Cushings lived in Boston, where John was a successful merchant. Olive was fifteen at the time of her marriage in 1773, and John was fifteen years older. Olive received General Lafayette, whom she had met in Boston during the war, on his visit to South Berwick in 1825. Elizabeth Wallingford was the third wife and widow of Colonel Thomas Wallingford, a wealthy merchant of Somersworth, New Hampshire. Elizabeth and Thomas had two children, Olive and Samuel, who died in battle off the English coast while fighting with John Paul Jones during the Revolution. Samuel's son, George Washington Wallingford, became a lawyer and moved to Kennebunk in 1800. His home there still stands and is now Wallingford Farm and Garden. The Cushing house remained in the family until the death of Charles Cushing Hobbs, Esq., when it was bought by the Town of South Berwick in 1920 as a site for a new school. The house was sold at public auction in 1924 for $325 to C.H. Stewart of Portsmouth, who took the house down, probably for salvage and resell. The home had been a famous and noted architectural landmark in its day, and its destruction was a great loss to the town. *Courtesy of Old Berwick Historical Society.*

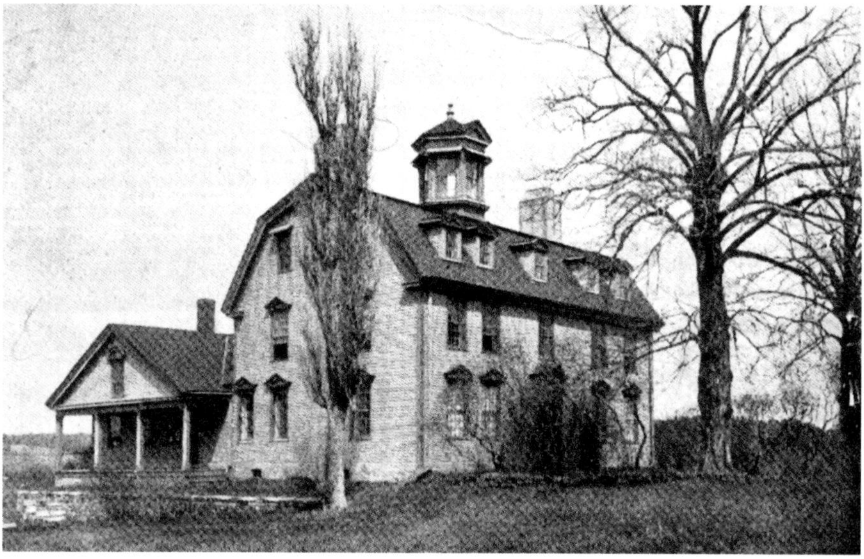

Sparhawk house, at Kittery Point, was a large, nineteen-room Georgian-style home built circa 1745 by William Pepperrell for his daughter Elizabeth as a wedding present upon her marriage to Nathaniel Sparhawk. Elizabeth and Nathaniel had four sons who were all Royalists and fled to England at the start of the Revolution but returned after the war ended. Horace Mitchell bought the home at the turn of the century and lived there until his death in 1922. Mitchell served in the House of Representatives and was also a teacher and postmaster. He was well known nationally for his abilities in organizing corporations, and he belonged to over five hundred corporations in Maine, whose total holdings were more than $1 billion. At the time, John D. Rockefeller only belonged to corporations worth half that amount. Mitchell's son, also named Horace, inherited the home and carved the property up into house lots and sold off some of the woodwork in the house. Strawberry Banke Museum acquired the home, and it was believed that the historic and architecturally important house would be moved to the museum in Portsmouth, New Hampshire. Instead, Strawberry Banke saved some moldings and paneling and then had the home demolished and the debris burned in 1967.

Opposite top: The Brackett House was demolished in 1938 for construction of a new and larger town hall for the town of Berwick. Built in the early 1800s, this three-story brick Federal-style home featured a store on the right side and living quarters on the left. Sabra Brackett inherited the home from her sister Hannah Cowell in 1874. Brackett sold to Casper Marshall, who owned the house until 1920. *Courtesy of Town of Berwick Collection.*

Opposite bottom: This Sanford home was famous for the towering elm on its front lawn. It was the home of George H. Nowell for many years. His store, Nowell and Libby, occupied the block where Shaw's Hardware is now located. The Nowell House stood where the Main Street entrance to the Mid-Town Mall is now located. It was torn down in 1947 to make way for a new First National Store.

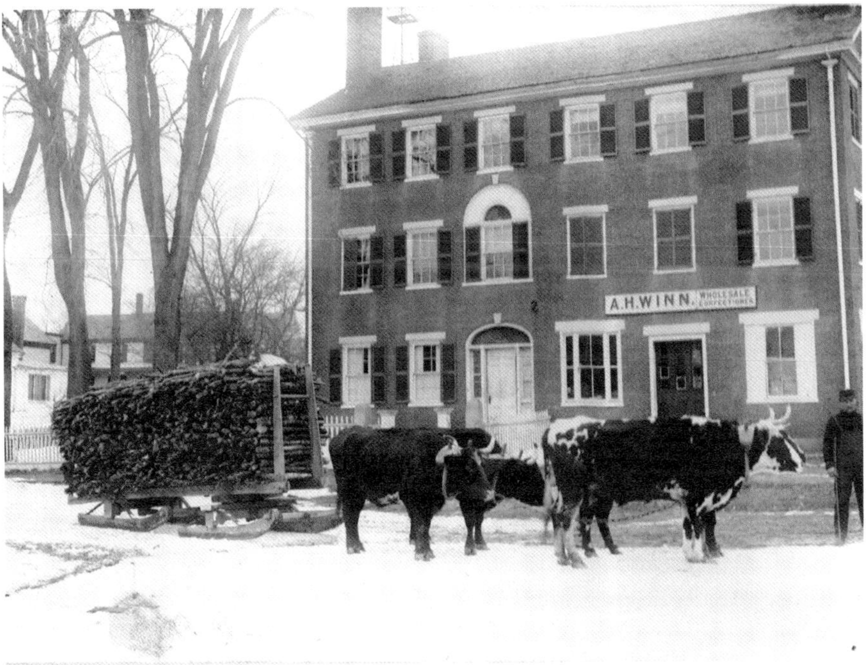
A.H.WINN.
WHOLESALE

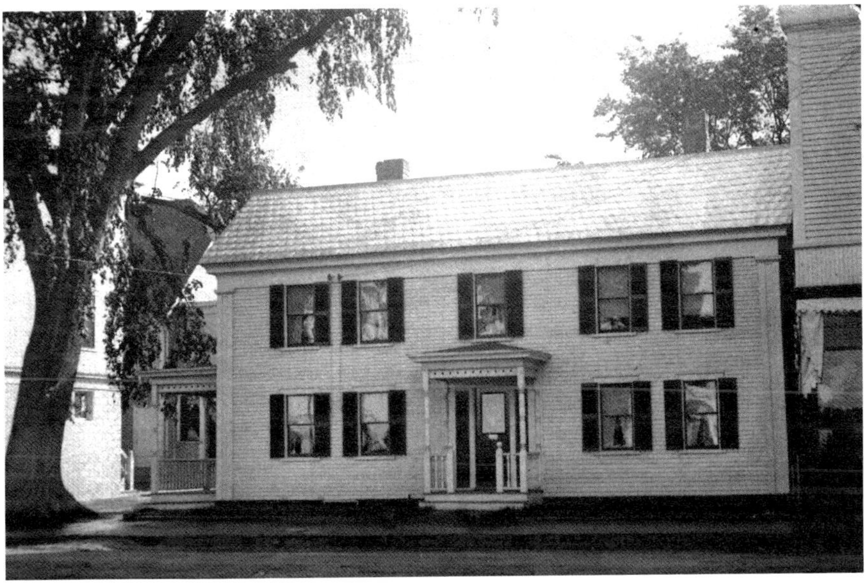

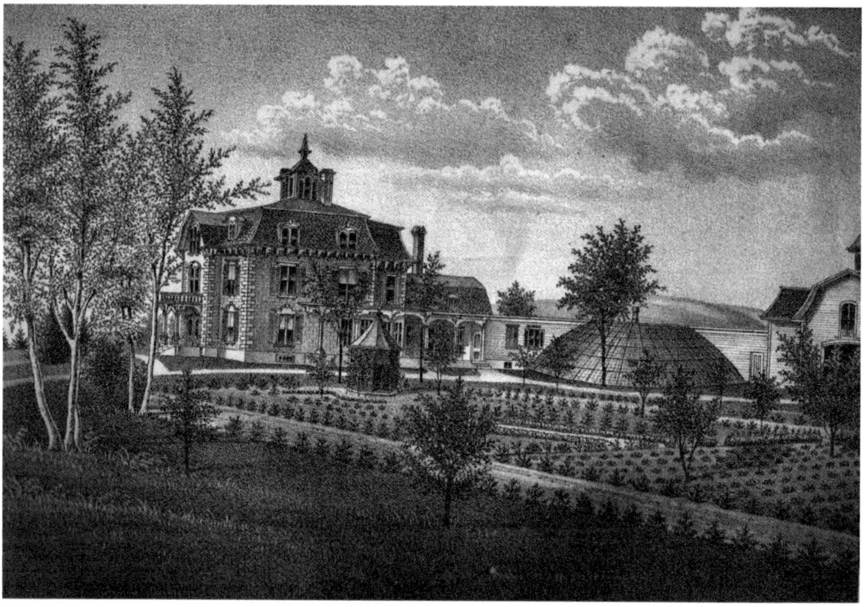

John Holmes Burleigh was a politician, sailor, banker and owner of the Great Works Woolen Mill. He died on December 5, 1877. His home, shown here, was located in South Berwick next to the Berwick Academy. It was built sometime after 1860 and burned circa 1895. *From* History of York County.

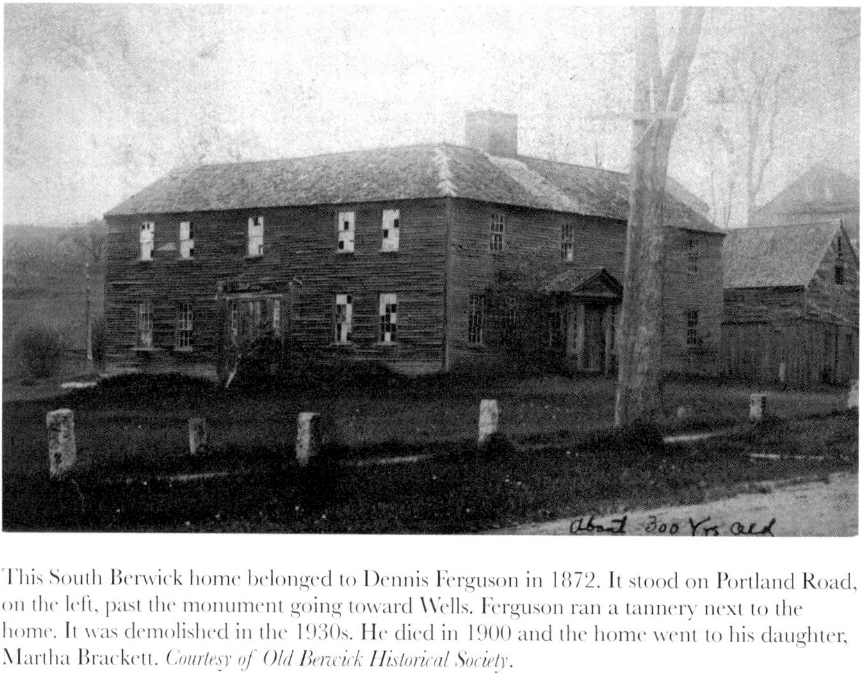

This South Berwick home belonged to Dennis Ferguson in 1872. It stood on Portland Road, on the left, past the monument going toward Wells. Ferguson ran a tannery next to the home. It was demolished in the 1930s. He died in 1900 and the home went to his daughter, Martha Brackett. *Courtesy of Old Berwick Historical Society.*

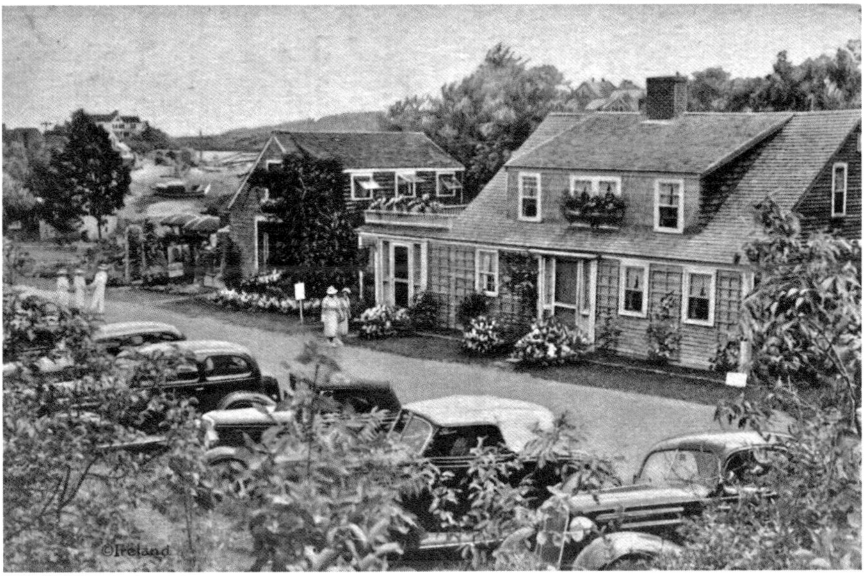

This Ogunquit home, on the right, was believed to have been built circa 1730 by John Littlefield and remained in the Littlefield family until 1922, when it was moved to Perkins Cove. It became part of the Whistling Oyster Restaurant, shown on the left, in 1929, when Helen E. Ryan and Joy Hawley bought it and opened a Christmas shop. Bette Davis once rented the apartment on the second floor. It burned in August 1976.

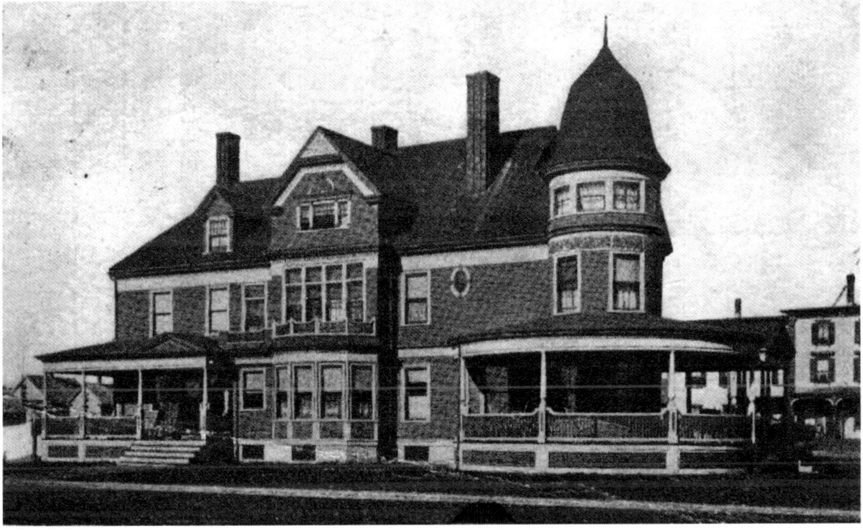

The Louis Bertrand Goodall house stood about where the Sunset Towers is located today in Sanford. Goodall was the son of Thomas Goodall, founder of the Goodall Mills, which L.B. Goodall ran with his brothers after their father died. He married Rose V. Goodwin in 1877, and this home was most likely built at that time or soon after. It was demolished about 1945.

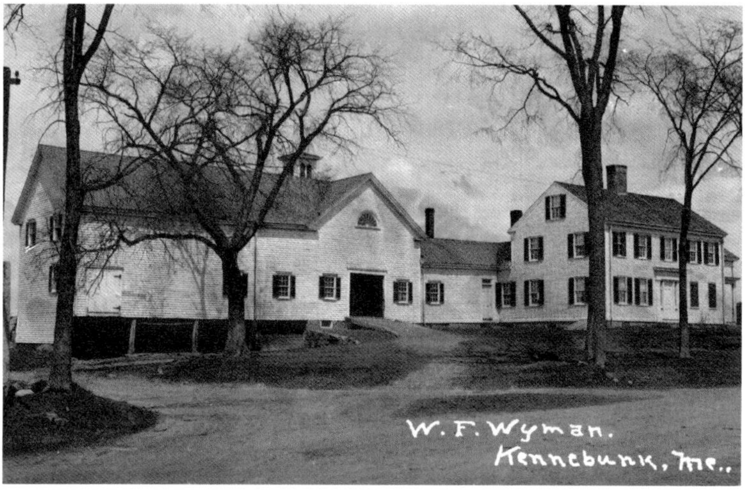

This once attractive home still stands but is almost unrecognizable today, as it has been covered in asbestos and plastic siding. It is located in Arundel, next to Walkers Lane, on Route 1. It was once owned by Moses Nason, who operated a carding mill behind the house. Charles Walker was the next owner, and he sold it to W.T. Wyman in 1910. The left side of the barn was removed and the shutters are gone as well. It was last used as the Arundel Meadows Inn.

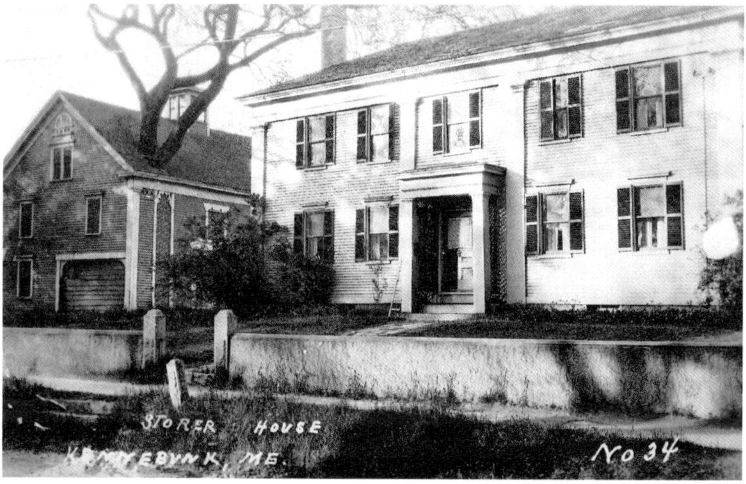

The Storer Mansion, in Kennebunk, still stands, but the famous barn with the tree growing through it was razed in 1929. The barn was a landmark for years, and according to a period newspaper article, Colonel Storer was such a great lover of trees that when he built his barn he didn't want to cut the tree down so he built around it. Later, Ethel Dunn bought the home and had a barn moved from Sanford and rebuilt around another tree on the property to recreate the original barn.

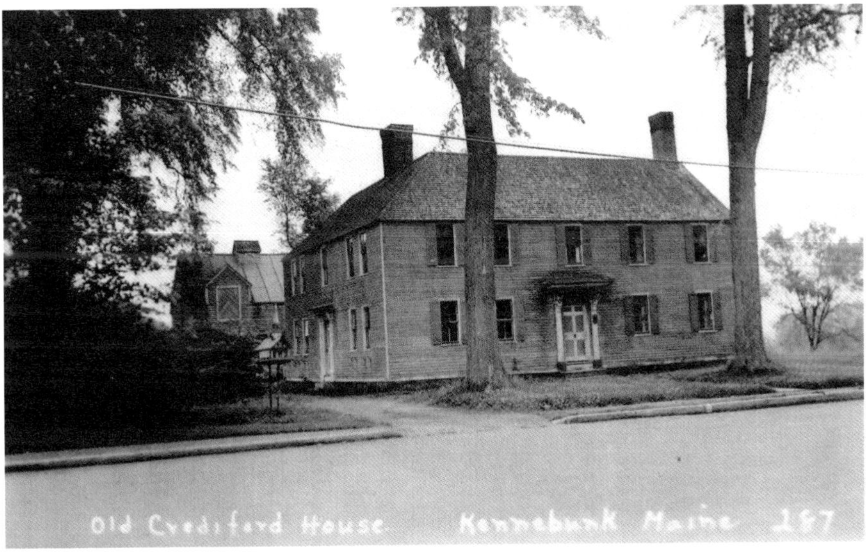

The Kimball-Crediford house stood on Summer Street in Kennebunk, where the police department is now located. It was built circa 1760 by James Kimball, a blacksmith, who was an early settler in Kennebunk. Annie Crediford, owner and editor of the *Enterprise* newspaper in Kennebunk, bought the house in the early 1900s. She sold the house to the United States government in 1937 and it was demolished for a new post office.

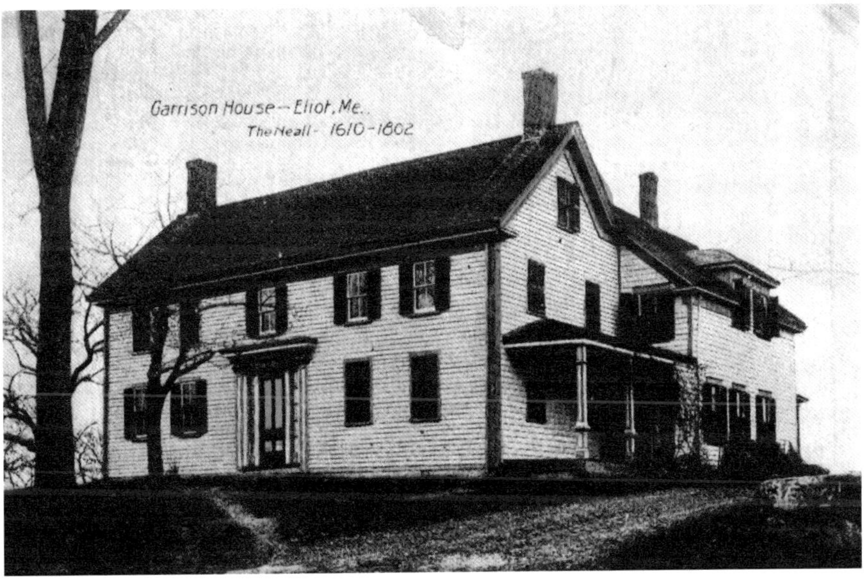

The Neall Garrison House stood on Goodwin Road in Eliot and this postcard suggests that the house was built in 1610, which seems unlikely since the Pilgrims didn't arrive in New England until 1621. Some part of an early home could have been incorporated into a later house when it was built, which was very common. This home burned on February 16, 1919.

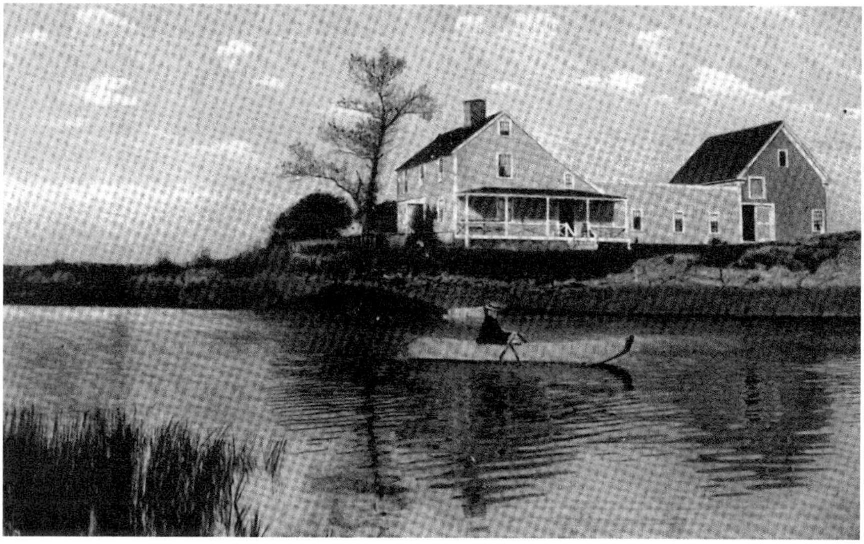

The Samuel Jordan home at Biddeford Pool, built circa 1717, was considered to have been the oldest home in the Biddeford-Saco area before it burned in 1960. Jordan ran a store out of his home and was considered to have been a principal leader in the development of Biddeford. The house survived the Indian wars because it was protected by a strong stone wall. It was later owned by the Goldwaite family.

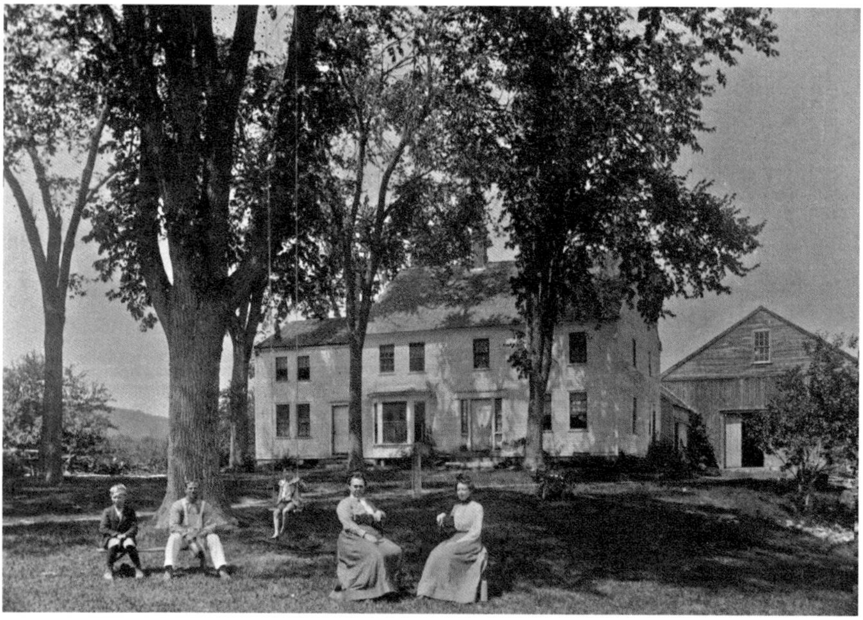

This home was owned in the 1880s by Dr. John Moulton and stood in Limington village. The people in this image may be members of his family. Ed Brunk owned the home when it burned down in February 1927. *Courtesy of Limington Historical Society.*

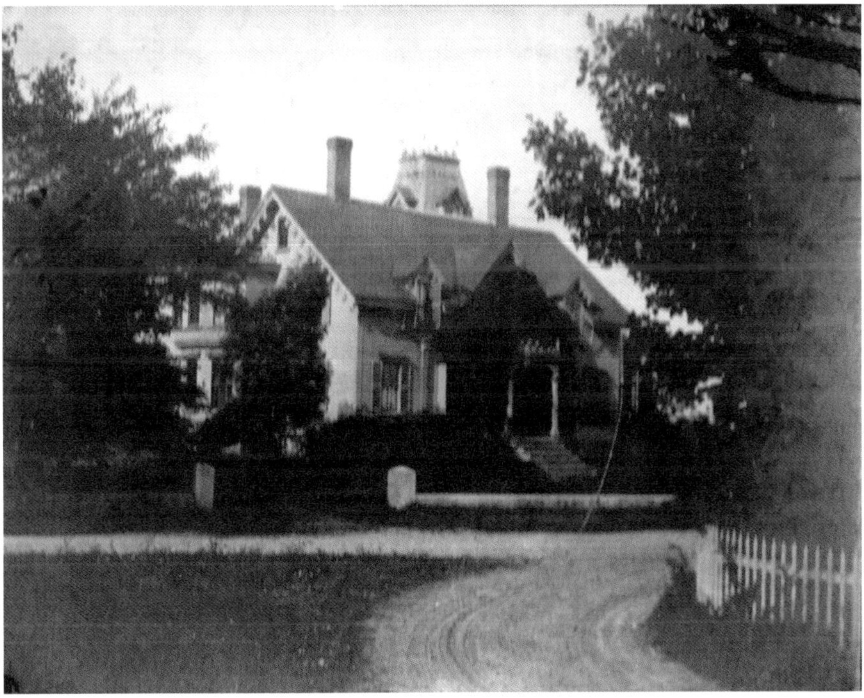

This Eliot home was owned by inventor Moses Gerrish Farmer and his wife, social reformer Hannah Tobey Shapleigh. It started out as a Greek Revival–, Cape-style home, and after they purchased it in the early 1880s, they expanded and remodeled the house to become the rambling Victorian-style mansion seen here. They named the property Bittersweet-in-the-Fields. Farmer was originally from Eliot and was serving as a professor of electrical science and a consultant to the U.S. Navy in Rhode Island. He and his daughter were in poor health and the family decided to return to Eliot. The idea for the name of the property supposedly came from the fact that they felt "bitter" about leaving their Rhode Island life behind, but it was sweet to be living in such a tranquil spot as Eliot.

Moses Grant Farmer was a pioneer telegraph operator and inventor of the nineteenth century and is credited with inventing the fire alarm and electric trolley. He invented several forms of the incandescent electric light twenty years before Thomas Edison patented his light bulb. While living in Salem, Massachusetts, Farmer lit the parlor of his home with incandescent lamps. This was the first house in the world to be lit by electricity. With his partner, William Wallace, Farmer invented an early dynamo that powered a system of arc lights that were exhibited at the Centennial Exhibition of 1876 in Philadelphia. This display apparently inspired Thomas Edison to work on an improved incandescent light. Farmer and his wife Hannah were spiritualists and believed that Farmer's inventions were given to him by God and that he should not seek wealth. Because of those beliefs, he didn't take credit for any of his inventions and is largely forgotten today. *Courtesy of Eliot Baha'i Archives.*

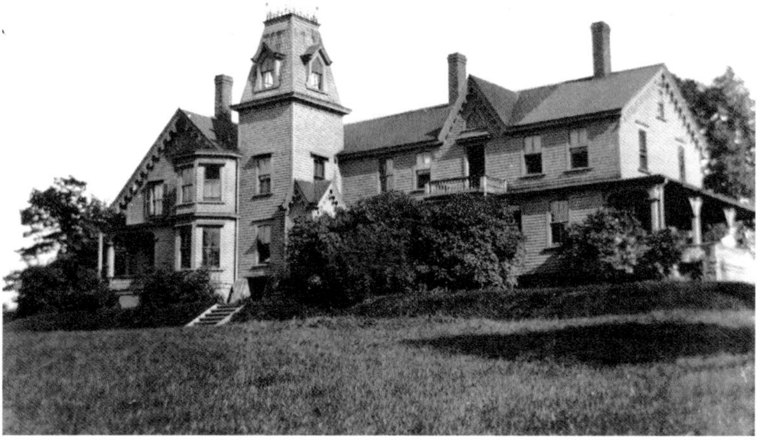

Another view of Bittersweet-in-the-Fields showing the extent of the alterations that the Farmers made. Hannah Tobey Shapleigh Farmer was a social reformer who was involved in the abolition and women's rights movements. Hannah founded Rosemary Cottage in Eliot as a place for inner-city women and their children to visit for a few weeks each summer. Sarah, their only child, inherited Bittersweet-in-the-Fields and it burned to the ground in 1904. *Courtesy of Eliot Baha'i Archives.*

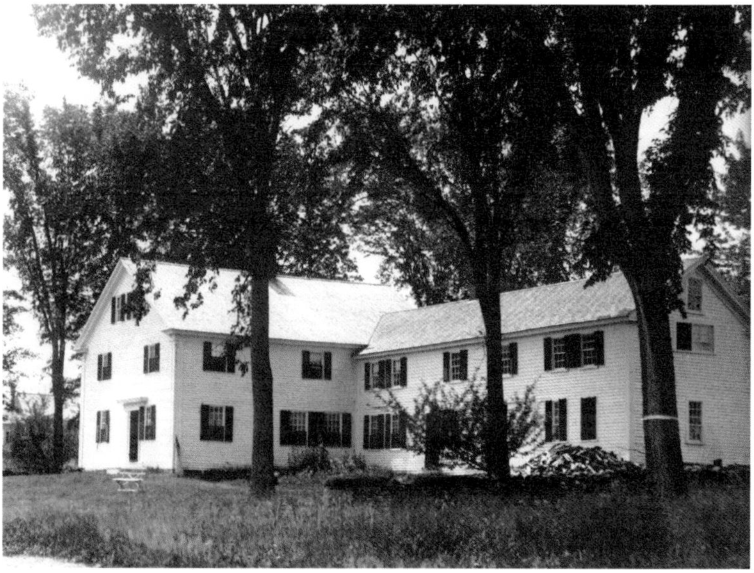

The Benjamin Thompson home was built by 1811 and stood on Maplewood Road, in Newfield. After Benjamin, the house was owned by his son Daniel and then by Daniel's son Usher B. Thompson. When Usher and his wife Sarah died, their adopted daughter Edith and her husband, Frank A. Page, made it their summer home. It burned down in the fire of 1947. *Courtesy of Sanford-Springfield Historical Society.*

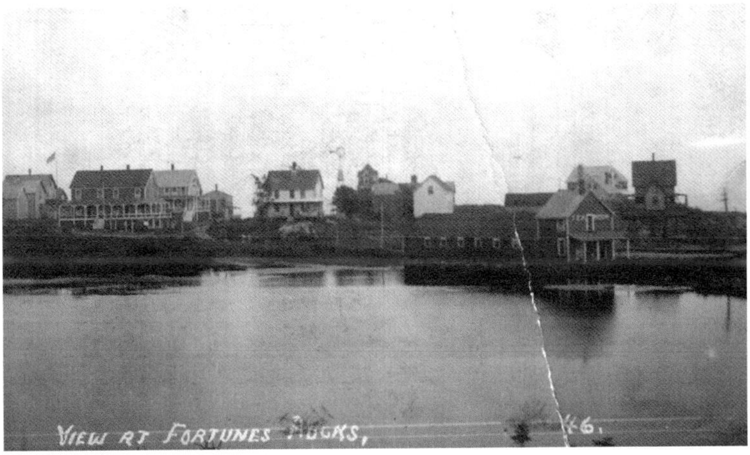

This image of Fortune's Rock, Biddeford, dates to circa 1915 and shows Berry Point (also called Haines Point) and the cottages and outbuildings that were built there. The Berry family, two brothers, built some of the first cottages at Fortune's Rock. The large building on the water was used as a community center and at various times housed a tearoom and bowling alley. Fortune's Rock was named after the Fortune family who once owned the land that W.C. Bryant bought in 1872. He divided the land into lots for summer cottages and hotels. All of these buildings burned down in the October 1947 forest fire.

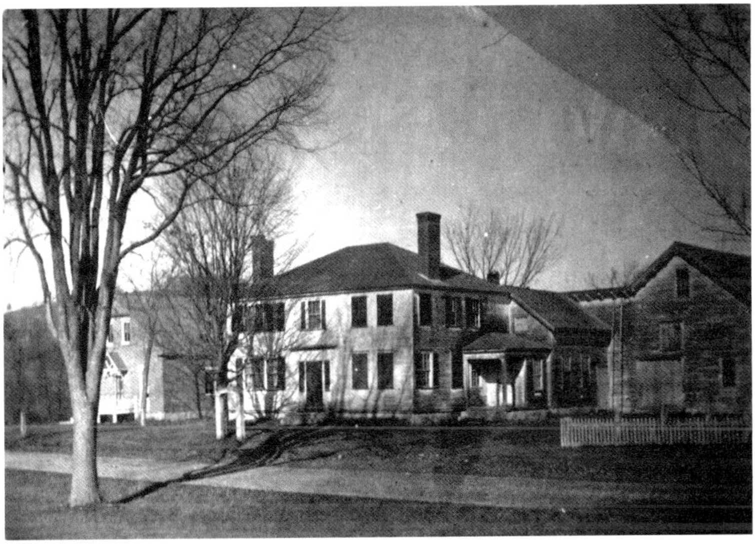

Nathan Clifford built his home in Newfield circa 1835. It stood opposite the current town hall and library on Route 11. Clifford lived here with his family until moving to Portland in 1849. The barn was taken down in 1940 and the home burned down in the fire of 1947. The brick schoolhouse, just visible to the left, was built between 1854 and 1856. It was converted to a home in 1898; it too burned down in 1947. *Courtesy of Newfield Historical Society.*

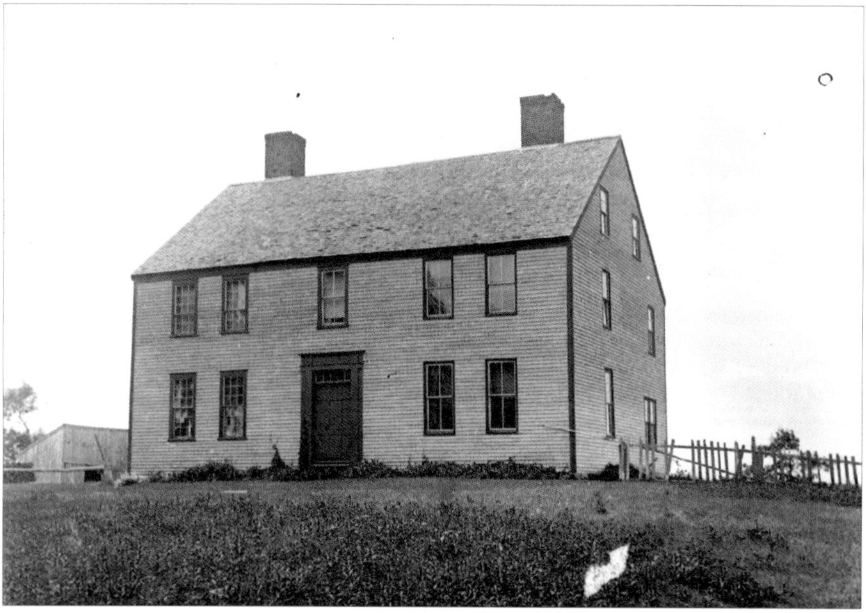

The Jordan house is located at Biddeford Pool and is seen here in an 1888 photograph. The house has been dated to circa 1740, and it was originally owned by Judge Rishworth Jordan, whose father was Samuel Jordan. While the building still stands and is part of the University of New England campus, it has been savagely altered and little but the frame and only one room of fine Georgian paneling remains in what was an important early landmark. In 1902, it was remodeled into a Colonial Revival–style mansion with a porte-cochère added to the side and other "improvements" to the interior. In 1931, it was sold to the Sisters of the Presentation of Mary and they added a large addition to the back and later a third floor. They ran a school out of the building known as the Stella Maris School. In 1962, St. Francis College bought the property and remained there until the school became secular. In this photograph you can see that the windows were being changed over to the two-over-two sash from the multi-pane original sash, a common practice at the time. *Courtesy of McArthur Library.*

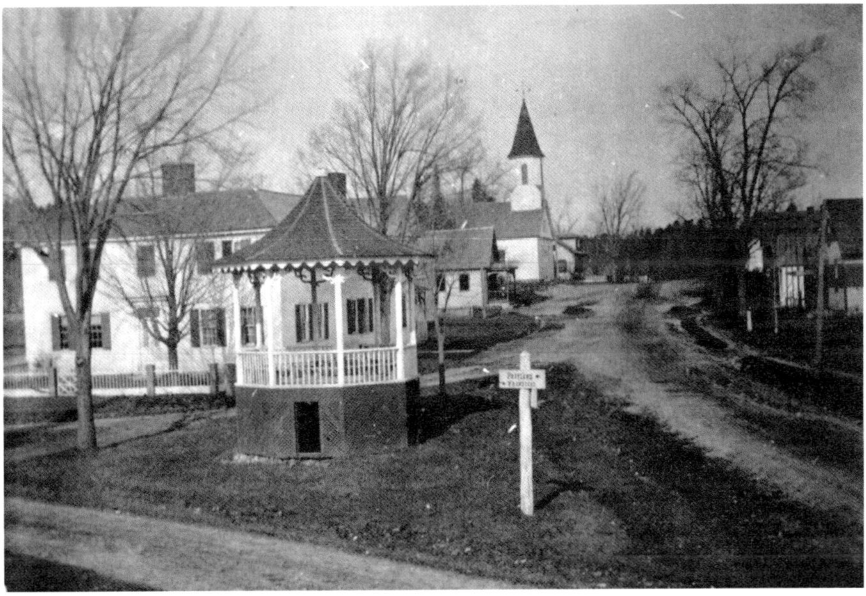

The Falker-Ayers house stood on the corner of Elm and Water Streets in Newfield. Nathaniel Falker married Martha Borne Ayer and later moved into this home built by her grandfather, Dr. James Ayers, in 1812. Falker, who was once a sea captain, died in 1919. This home, the bandstand built in 1878 and the post office behind it all burned down in the fire of 1947. Congregationalists, Baptists and Free Will Baptists built the church in the background in 1833. After being vacant for a number of years, it was renovated into an auditorium in 1913. It also burned down in 1947. *Below*: The ruins of the Falker home, October 1947. *Courtesy of Newfield Historical Society*.

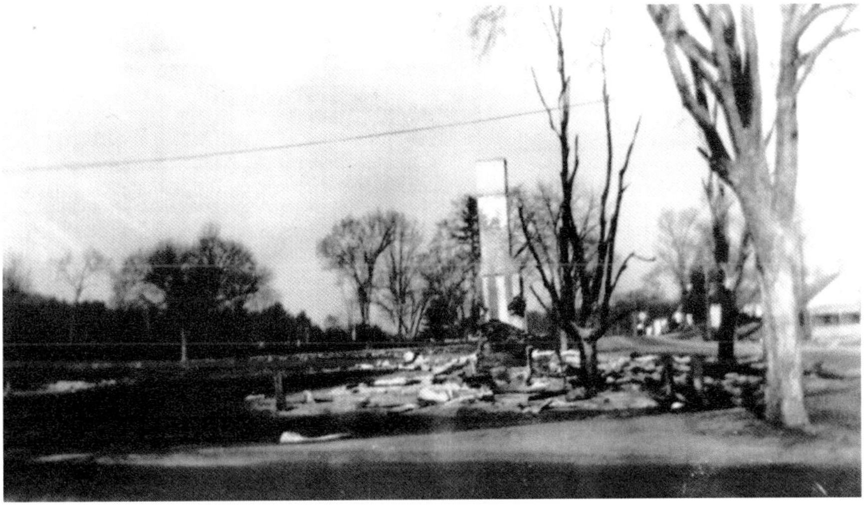

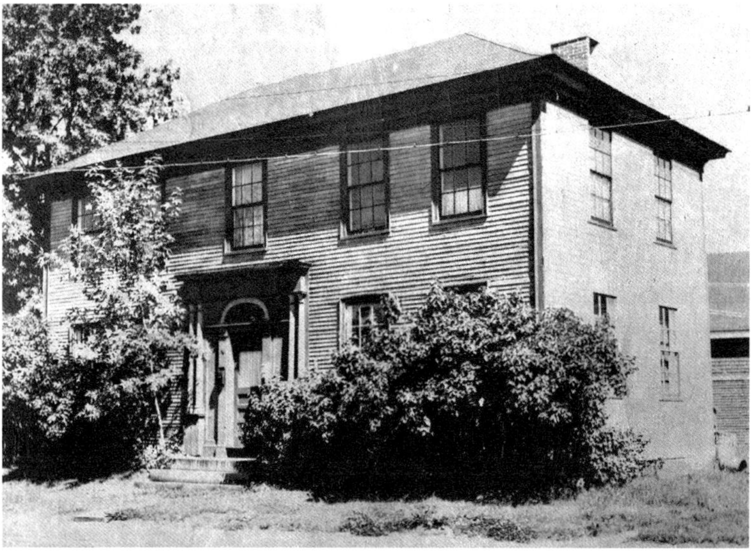

Captain Moses Bradbury's home stood on Spring's Island in Biddeford where Deering Lumber's parking lot is now located. His home was the first house built on the island in 1795. Designed in the Federal style, Bradbury and Seth Spring operated sawmills on the island, which is surrounded by the Saco River. The house was dismantled in 1973 by Mr. and Mrs. Loren Prentice and was rebuilt at Allen's Point in Harpswell, Maine. *Courtesy of McArthur Library.*

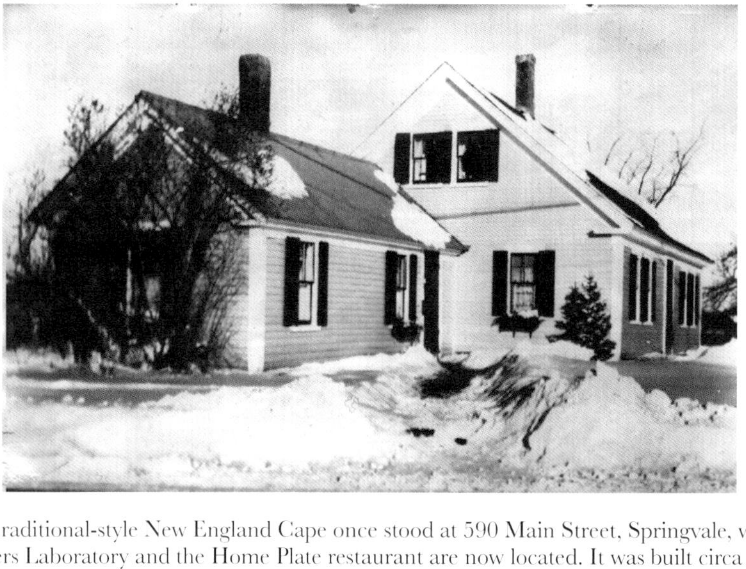

This traditional-style New England Cape once stood at 590 Main Street, Springvale, where Demers Laboratory and the Home Plate restaurant are now located. It was built circa 1770 by Jonathan Adams and was the first house in that part of town. Adams fought in the Battle of Louisburg under William Pepperrell in 1745. His son, Jonathan Jr., fought at Lexington and Bunker Hill during the Revolution. Joseph Whitman bought the home in 1817. It was demolished in 1968. *Courtesy of Harland Eastman.*

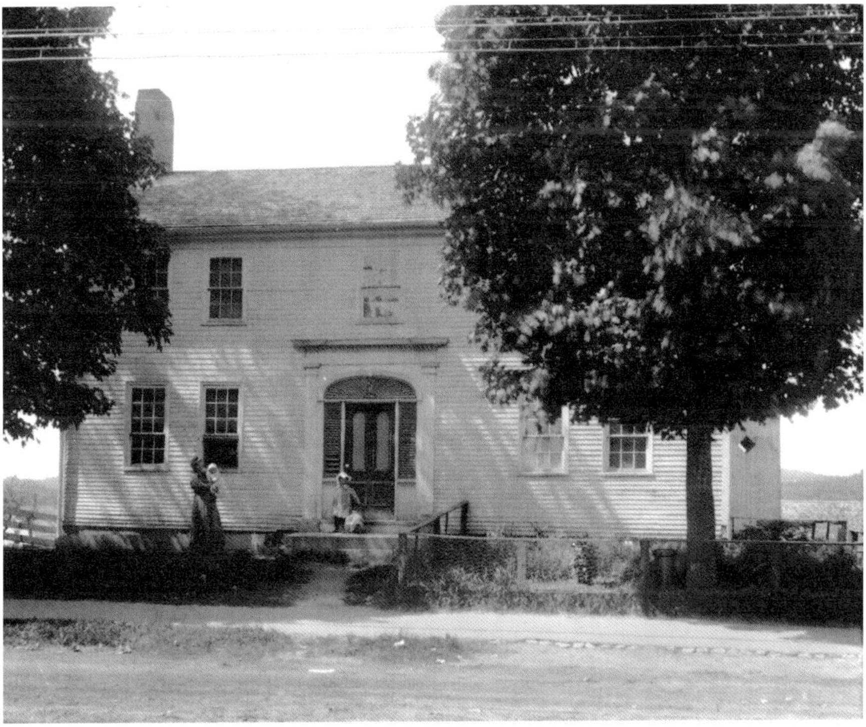

Shapleigh Tavern, in Sanford, was built about 1828 by James B. Shapleigh. It stood across from the Movie Gallery, where Kennebunk Savings Bank is now located. In 1849, the Tebbetts family bought the tavern for their private home and operated a bakery next door. Both buildings were bought by William Bachelder in 1919 and demolished for a new brick garage called Sanford Garage. *Courtesy of Sanford-Springvale Historical Society.*

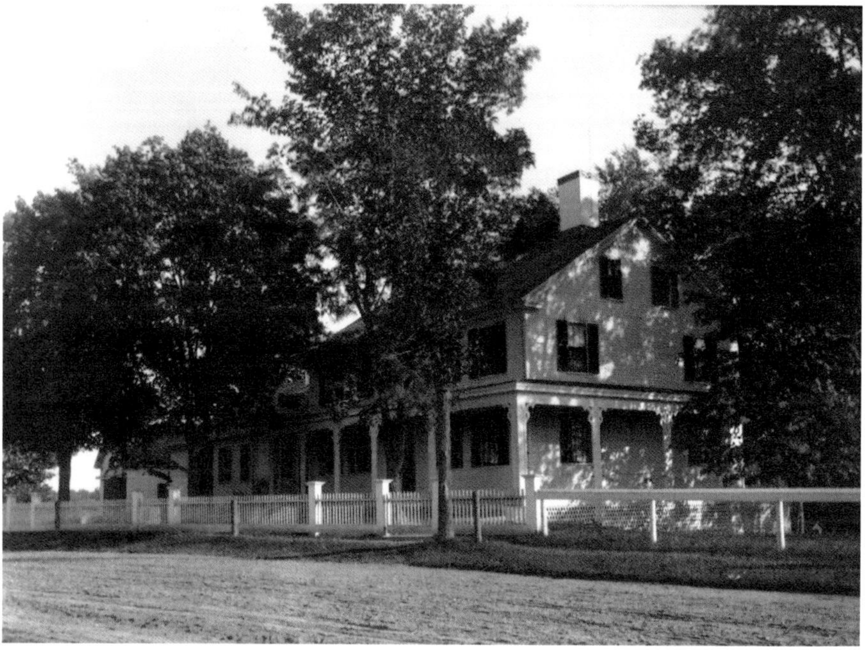

This beautiful home, which stood in the heart of Alfred village, on Saco Road, was originally owned by William Green Conant. Conant was a local merchant and ran a store in the village for over forty years. Eugene W. Hewett, who worked for the Sanford National Bank, owned the home for many years after Conant. It's hard to imagine anyone wanting to mutilate this attractive and well-kept home, but that's what happened. In 1977, new owners bought the home and set out to destroy it, and they did a very good job, too. They tore off all the additions and porches, ripped out all the windows and replaced the roof with a low, hipped roof. They installed small, fake diamond windows, one on each side of the front door and three above. Then they ripped off the original clapboards and covered the house in dark brown shingles. It was a hideous mess and an eyesore for almost thirty years. Why people do these things to old homes is beyond reason; if you don't like a home, don't buy it. If you want everything straight and true, and windows and doors that open freely, build a new house. Leave the old house to someone who loves old buildings and will preserve it. The Conant home burned a few years ago and couldn't be saved. A new home was built on the old foundation, which survived the fire. *Courtesy of Sanford-Springvale Historical Society.*

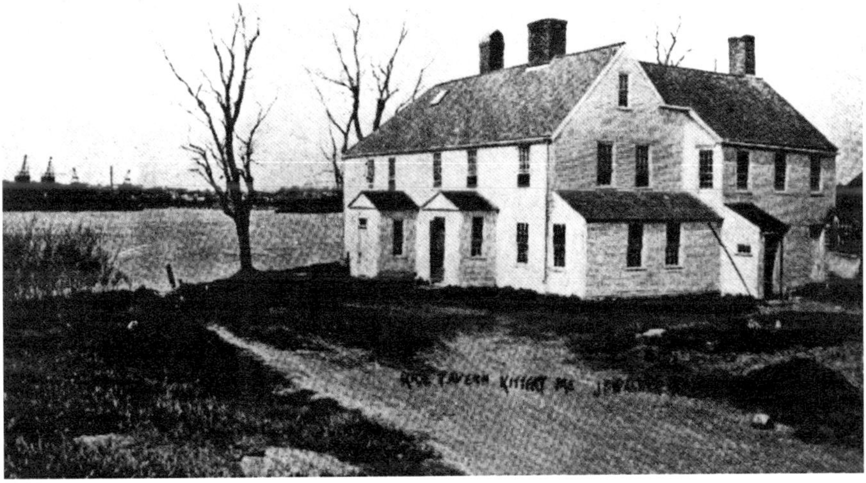

Rice Tavern stood off Water Street on the Piscataqua River in Kittery. The Rice family operated the tavern and a ferry there until the first bridge was constructed over the river in 1822. Ann Elizabeth Rice was the last member of the family to live there. When she died in 1874, her brother Alexander inherited the home. He died in 1877. The tavern was demolished in the early 1940s for new house construction.

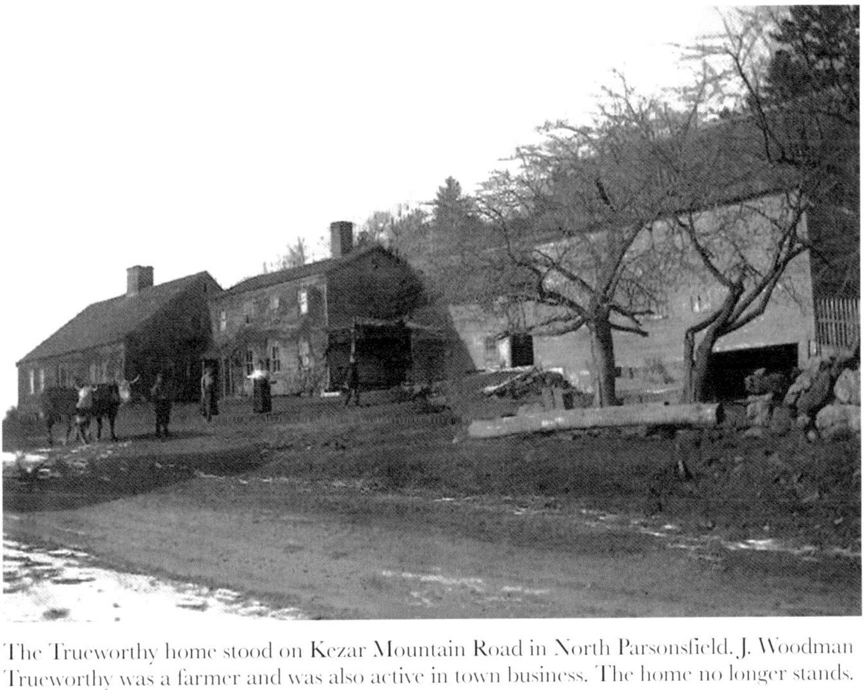

The Trueworthy home stood on Kezar Mountain Road in North Parsonsfield. J. Woodman Trueworthy was a farmer and was also active in town business. The home no longer stands. *Courtesy of Parsonsfield Porter Historical Society.*

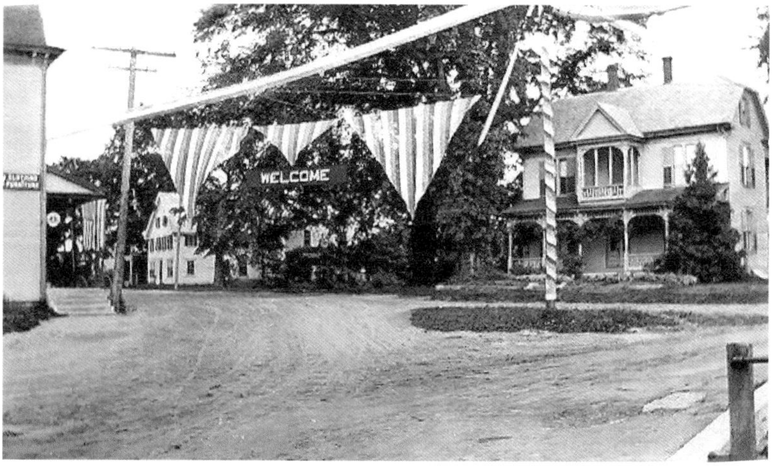

The Bullock house stood where the Parsonsfield Post Office is located today. Gideon M. Randall, a merchant, built this stylish home in 1831 and it was later owned by the Jeremiah Bullock family. The home burned down sometime after 1927. The building on the left was built by George W. Towle circa 1885 and still stands today, minus the third floor, which was removed after a fire in 1937. *Courtesy of Parsonsfield Porter Historical Society.*

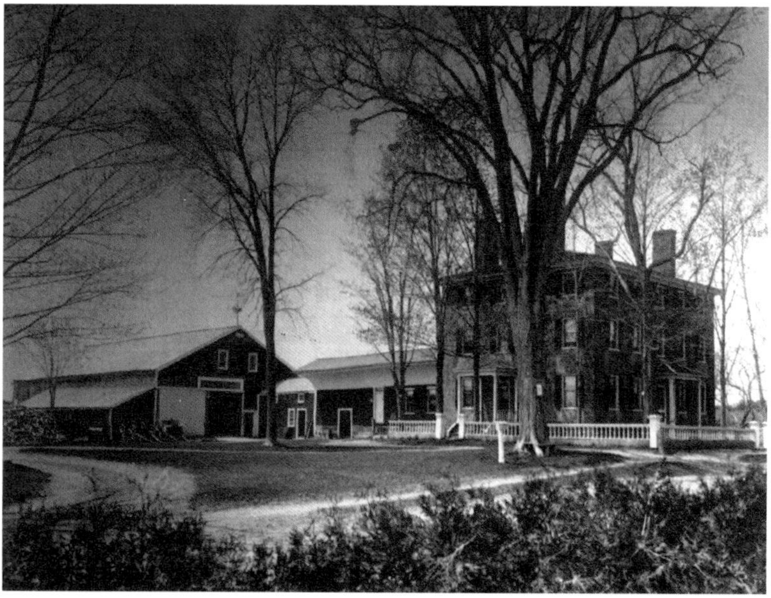

This fine brick, Federal, three-story home was built by Andrew Conant around 1800 in Alfred. He intended to use it as an inn, but those plans fell through, so he used it as his home. It contained a ballroom on the third floor. Conant was born in 1773 and was active in town politics and was a captain in the militia. The home burned down on March 2, 1969. *Courtesy of Sanford-Springvale Historical Society.*

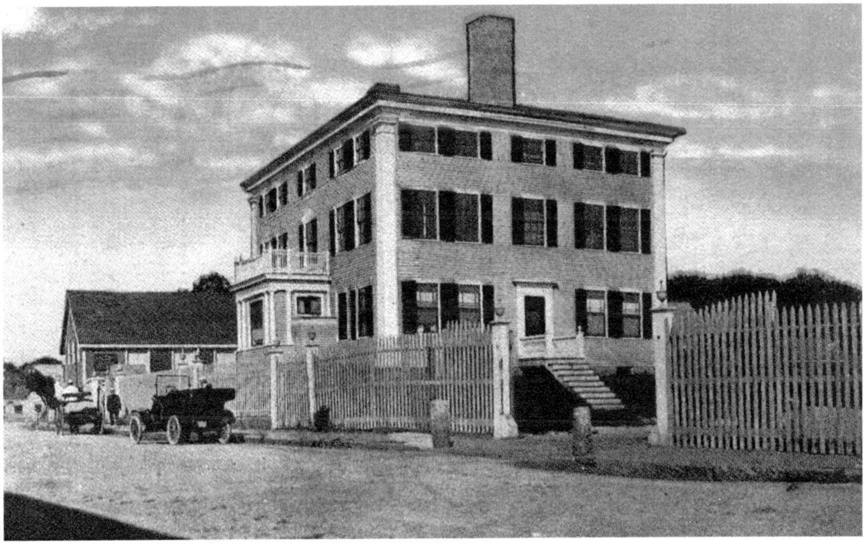

Spring Tavern in Biddeford sits on a small island in the middle of the Saco River and is connected to both Biddeford and Saco by two bridges. Captains Seth Spring and Moses Bradbury bought the island and a mill located there in 1794. In 1798, Spring constructed an elegant, three-story, Federal-style home, which he opened as a tavern and inn. It was there that he entertained General Lafayette in 1825. Spring Tavern still stands today but has suffered much abuse. Its decline began when the property was purchased by Joseph G. Deering in 1869. He constructed and operated several sawmills on the property and established what is known today as Deering Lumber, which now operates from the old Spring Tavern. The original staircase is gone, probably removed when the home was converted to apartments in 1895, and the first-floor rooms were gutted when it was converted to office and retail space for the lumber company. Its decline continued after the business was bought by Thomas Armstrong in 1958. A large retail addition was tacked onto the side of the historic building in 1980.

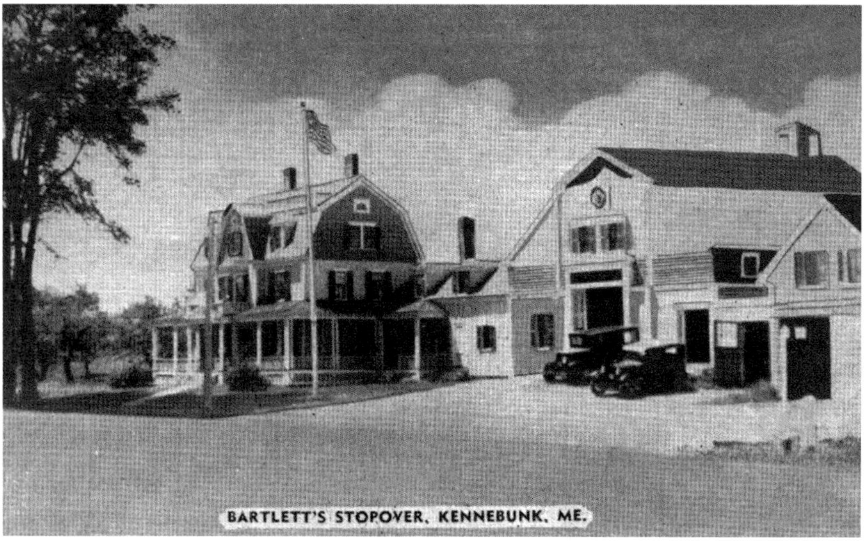

The William Bartlett home stood on Route 1 in Kennebunk, next to the Kennebunk River. His home started out as a typical New England Cape, which he had local architect William Barry redesign, turning it into the Colonial Revival mansion seen here. Later family members who inherited the home let it fall to ruin and it was burned for fire practice.

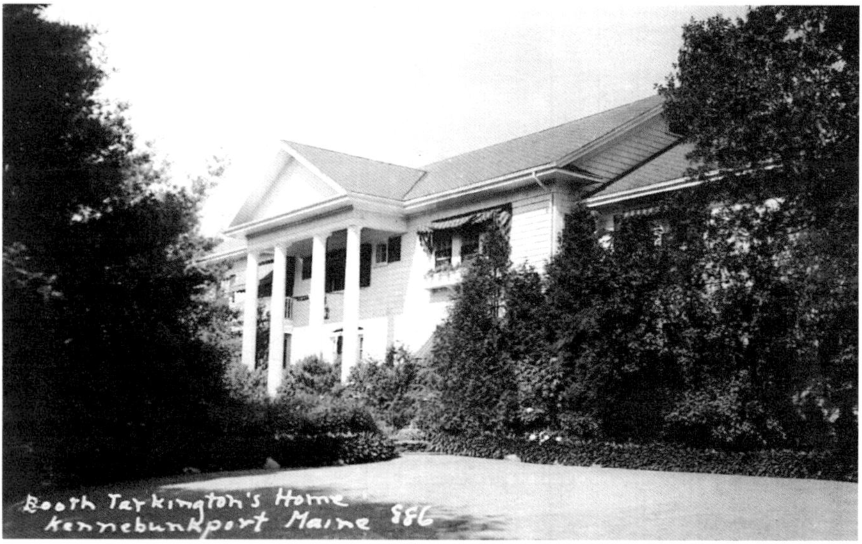

Booth Tarkington was born in Indiana and in the early twentieth century was a popular writer whose works were made into movies, like *The Magnificent Ambersons*. He came to Kennebunkport in 1903 for health reasons and made it his home, building this Colonial Revival home off Ocean Avenue in 1916. His home still stands but has been made into condominiums, and his library was gutted and turned into a garage.

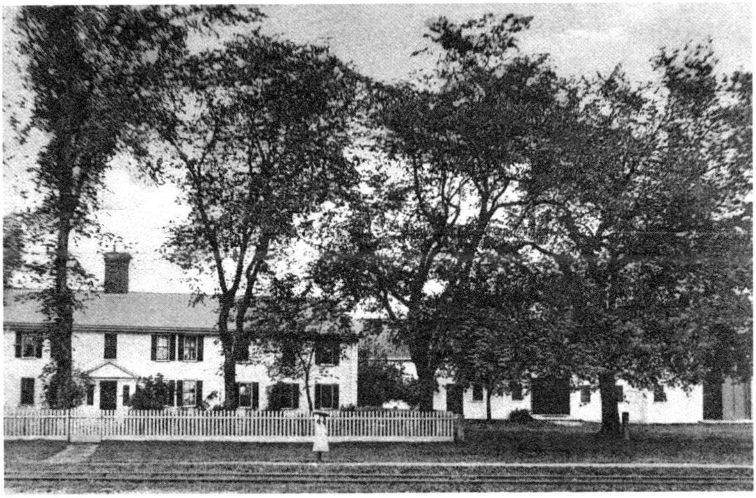

The Perkins-Howard farm in West Kennebunk was built circa 1785. Oliver Perkins bought the property in 1826, and around 1846 he opened it as a tavern. It still stands; however, several years ago a Biddeford contractor bought the historic home and gutted it. He removed all the original woodwork, staircase, windows, doors and destroyed historic wallpaper as well. This home is a good example of what not to do when rehabbing a historic home.

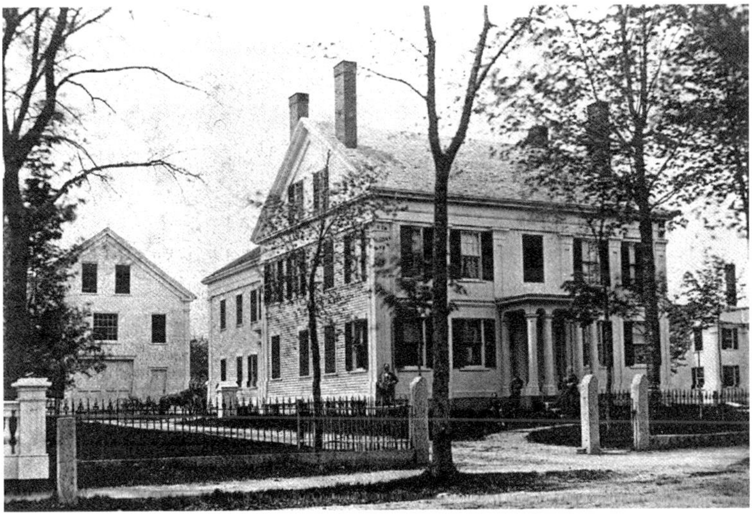

This Greek Revival home on Kennebunk's historic Summer Street still stands, but the barn in back was taken down many years ago for parking when the building was used as a Christian Science church. Today it is a private home. Barns are fast disappearing around York County, and around the country, as homeowners lack the funds to keep them in repair. These important landmarks, remnants of the county's farming legacy, are an important component of York County's landscape and need to preserved.

CHAPTER TWO

HOTELS AND MOTELS

The state of Maine is known as "Vacationland." The coastal towns of York County have long embraced this, as tourism has been the principal industry for over 150 years. Early visitors were drawn to the county's old homes and history, as well its sandy beaches, rocky coast, lakes and streams and, of course, the ocean. York County's first hotels were built in the 1850s, and these large, wooden buildings were constructed quickly and cheaply. The Passaconaway Hotel, for example, built in the town of York in 1892, was constructed in just over forty days. After the Civil War, developers like the Boston and Kennebunkport Seashore Company began purchasing land in Kennebunkport, which was sold cheaply because farmers felt it had no value. Such ventures established numerous summer resorts. The stock market panic of 1873 slowed development, but renewed economic conditions in the 1880s spurred a building boom.

Eventually, the early summer resorts of coastal York County would rank with those in Bar Harbor, Maine, and Newport, Rhode Island. York, Ogunquit, Kennebunk Beach and Kennebunkport attracted doctors, lawyers, professors, bankers, artists, writers and actors—a range of northeastern wealth. Old Orchard Beach was once considered equal to Kennebunkport and York, though its reputation changed in later years as amusement parks took over the town. Throughout its history, Old Orchard Beach was especially popular with tourists from Canada, many of whom still flock to the town beach each summer.

During the latter half of the nineteenth century, tourists traveled to coastal resort hotels to escape the heat in the cities. Depending on their economic situations, they would stay for the whole season or half the season. The hotels offered all the most modern conveniences available at the time for their guests. Wealthy visitors eventually built huge rambling cottages in the popular Shingle style, where they would stay for just two months each year. Guest houses, often someone's private home, could be rented at cheaper rates to provide a more personal atmosphere. The season was shorter then too—hotels opened for the Fourth of July and closed promptly at the end of August.

The large wooden hotels that were built posed other problems in the days before fire and building codes existed. They frequently caught fire, and when they did, there was little anyone could do to stop it in the days before modern fire equipment existed. Old Orchard Beach suffered a catastrophic fire on August 15, 1907, that destroyed most of the downtown area. Fires also occurred at Kennebunk Beach and Kennebunkport hotels, as well as in other towns. In York, the original Marshall House burned down and was replaced by a brick hotel with all the safety features available at the time. This continued into the twentieth century as surviving hotels aged and years of additions made them susceptible to fire. As the resort business began to die out after World War II, many of the surviving hotels were deliberately set on fire for the insurance money.

One of the contributors to the demise of the resort hotel in York County was the automobile. It changed the way Americans traveled, making it possible for tourists to visit several towns around the state instead of staying in one place. In the 1920s, the State of Maine rebuilt and widened Route 1 from Kittery to Bar Harbor. This, along with new technology in automobile construction, made it possible for cars to travel farther with fewer breakdowns. Campgrounds, motor courts, restaurants and gas stations were quickly built along the new highway, offering travelers inexpensive accommodations. The large hotels in York County tried to adapt by adding garages and car services, but the First World War, new tax laws and the Depression cut into business. When World War II began, many of the large resort hotels shut down for the duration because of rationing and lack of help. By the 1960s, slow business, new fire regulations and rising land values resulted in the demolition of some of the county's most elegant and famous hotels. Most were demolished to create lots for new homes and cottages.

The popularity of roadside cabins and restaurants waned faster than the popularity of the resort hotels. Motels gave guests a certain amount of anonymity, which often bred illegal activity. By the 1930s, Hollywood was making movies that featured motels as run-down, popular with criminals and located in seedy parts of towns and cities. As automobile technology improved, creating faster and safer cars that could travel farther on less gas and with fewer repairs, the need for so many roadside cabins declined. Some cabin owners turned to illegal activities to make money, operating gambling machines or renting rooms by the hour. In addition, new super highways, like the Maine Turnpike, which opened in 1947, and modern hotels based on the designs of Holiday Inn and Howard Johnson attracted the American traveler with clean, safe rooms and spelled the end of roadside motor courts. Some motels survive today, but most were lost to fire, road expansion or neglect. Many have disappeared so completely that today they survive only in memory, period postcards or old newspapers clippings.

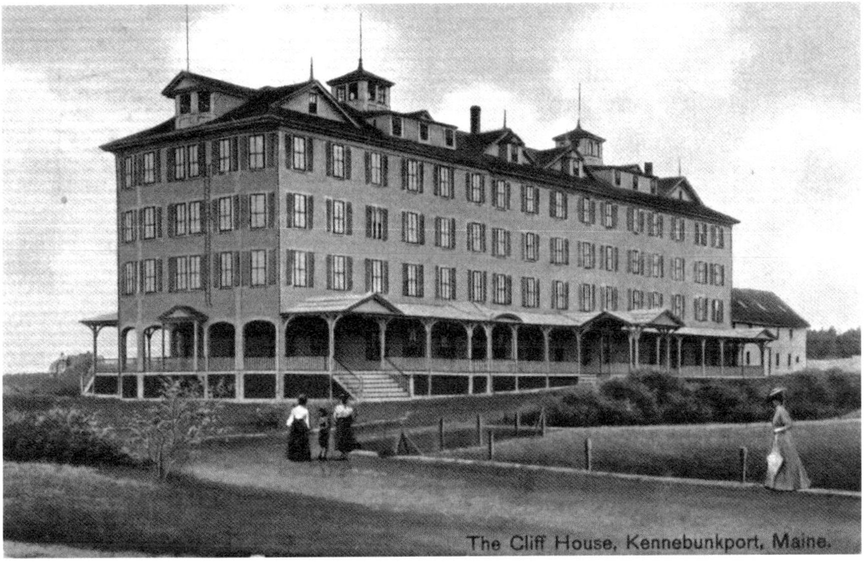

The Cliff House, located in Kennebunkport, was built in 1881 for B.F. Eldridge and was originally two stories with a mansard roof. It was enlarged in 1897 to four stories, doubling the size of the hotel.

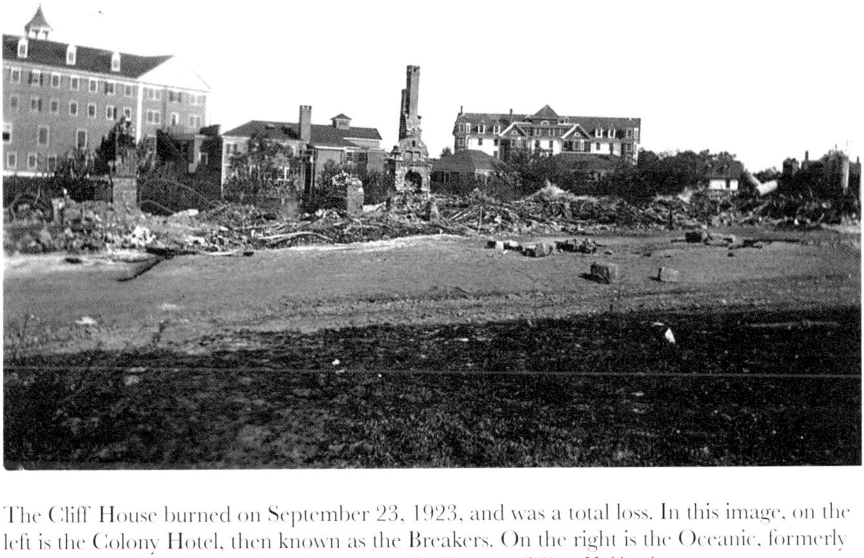

The Cliff House burned on September 23, 1923, and was a total loss. In this image, on the left is the Colony Hotel, then known as the Breakers. On the right is the Oceanic, formerly known as the Glen House; it no longer stands. *Courtesy of Greg Hubbard.*

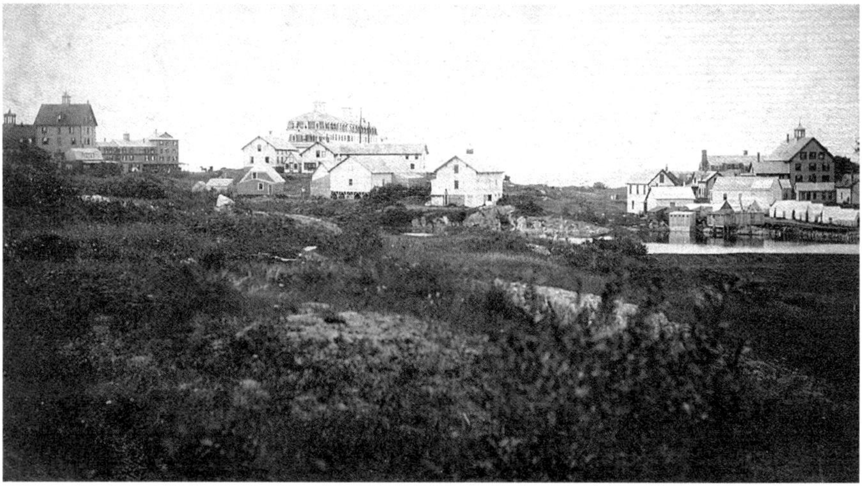

This image of Ocean Avenue in Kennebunkport was taken before the Ocean Bluff (center) burned down in January 1898. It was built in 1873 and business partners Simpson and Devnell operated it until it burned. The Colony Hotel was built on the site in 1908. The hotels seen here are (from right to left) the Riverside and, just visible behind that, the Arundel Inn. The buildings behind the Ocean Bluff were the stables and barns for the hotel. Next is the Cliff House, and the hotel with the two cupolas was the Glen House, which is still partially standing. *Courtesy of Greg Hubbard.*

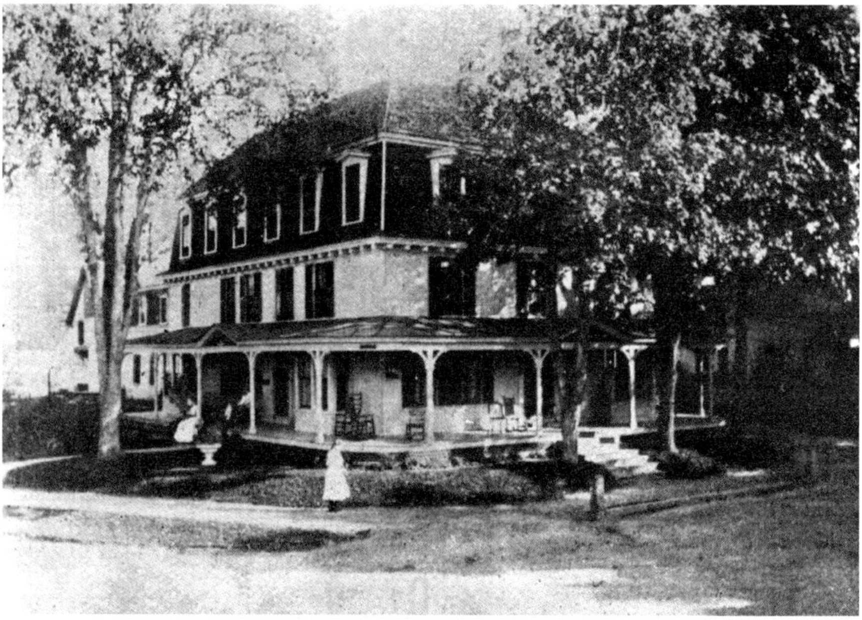

The Lincoln House in Cornish still stands but was altered and enlarged in the 1920s. Today it is known as the Cornish Inn.

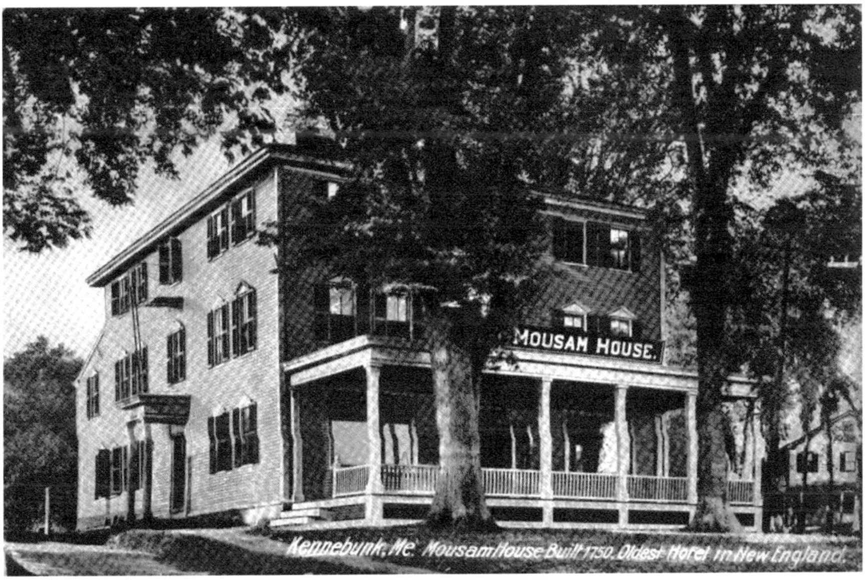

The original section of this hotel was built in Kennebunk about 1784 as a private home. In 1791, William Jefferds bought it and opened an inn. The front three-story section was added after 1800. President James Monroe dined here in 1817 and General Lafayette was entertained here in 1825. B.F. Goodwin moved the Mousam House to this location in 1861. In 1937, the historic inn was sold to Marshall Weeman, who demolished it for a gas station. The area around the inn, the intersection of York and High Streets and Brown Street was once filled with historic buildings, now gone. There was the Jefferds' home to the left of the Mousam House, razed in 1963 for N.T. Fox Lumber, now Deering Lumber. Above where the Dairy Queen now stands were two important homes: the Unitarian parsonage, built in 1797 by John Low, a deacon for the First Parish Church (now the First Parish Unitarian Church), and the Dimond Gilpatrick home, built in 1802. Both buildings were destroyed in 1979 by Paul Bedard for a parking lot. The destruction of these buildings was the greatest architectural and historical loss for the town of Kennebunk.

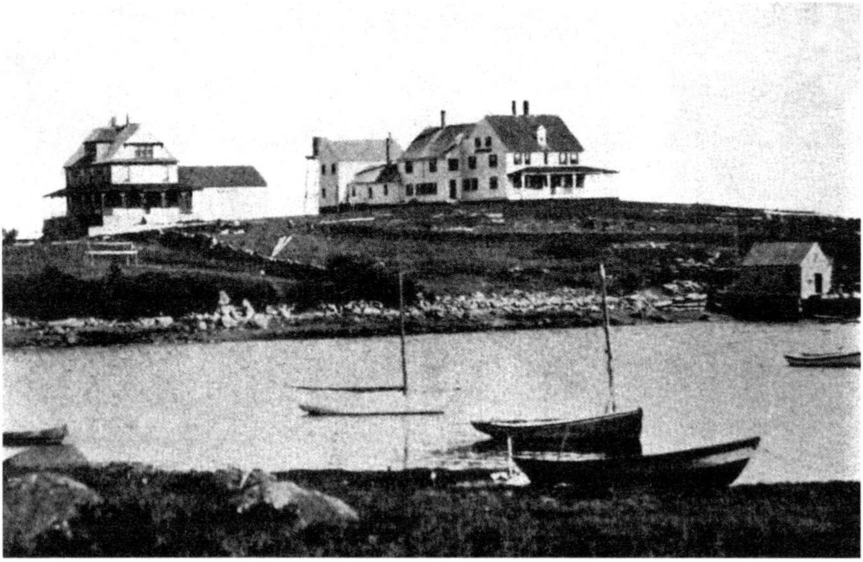

Stone Haven was a hotel located in Cape Porpoise on Pier Road, near Bickford Island. Clement Stone began taking in boarders in the 1880s and most likely gave the establishment its name. In 1898, the Cape Porpoise Land Company bought the building and remodeled and expanded the home into a full hotel. It closed by 1928 and burned down in April 1931. *Courtesy of Greg Hubbard.*

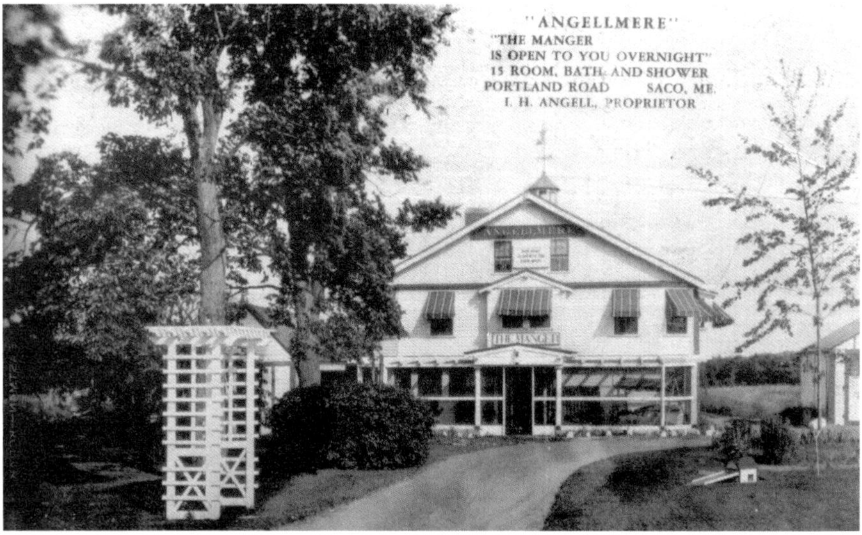

Isaac H. Angell purchased this building in 1926 and opened it as a seasonal inn called the Manger. It later became the Manger Motor Court. The building is still standing next to the Saco Drive-In, in Saco, but has been altered and is now used as a daycare center.

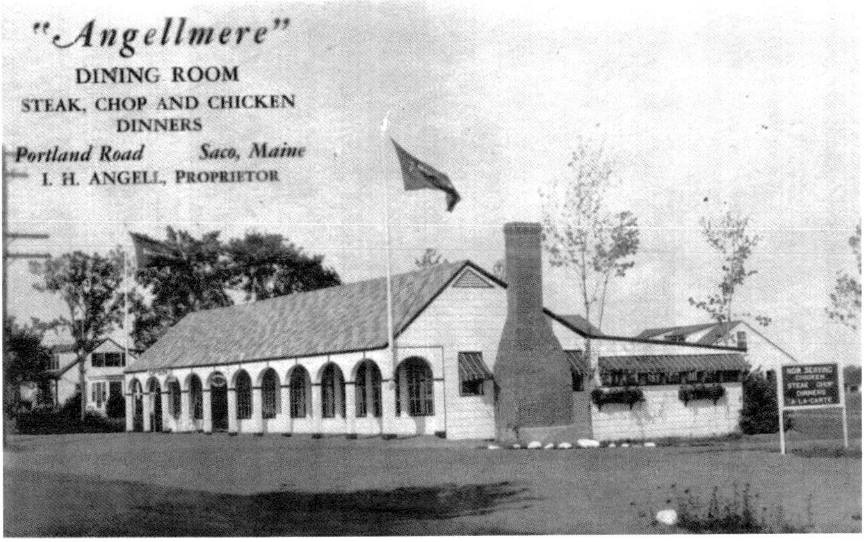

Isaac Harold Angell opened the Angellmere Restaurant in Saco next to his home in the 1930s. He sold it in 1948 but kept the inn next door. The restaurant no longer stands. The house just visible in the distance was demolished in 2007.

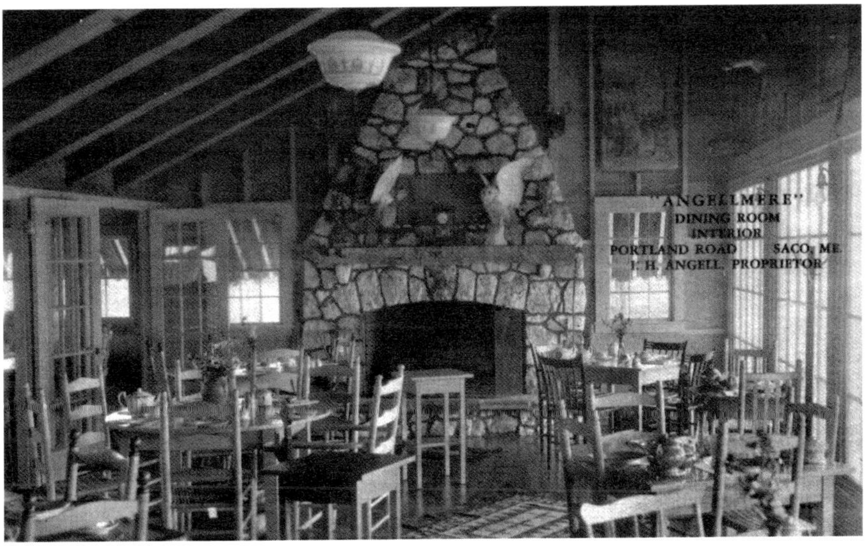

This is the interior of the Angellmere Restaurant, which stood next to the Saco Drive-In. As you can see, it was just a seasonal operation and the interior was unfinished and rustic.

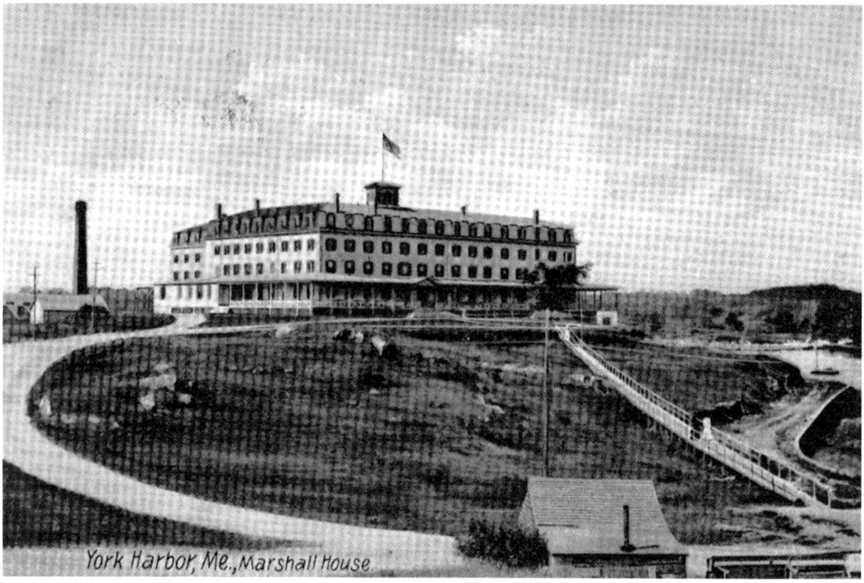

Nathaniel Grant Marshall built the Marshall House, shown here, in 1871 on Stage Neck Island in York. It opened up the town to tourism and helped create a summer resort equal to Newport and Bar Harbor. The large wooden hotel was painted yellow with white trim and green shutters. It burned down in 1916.

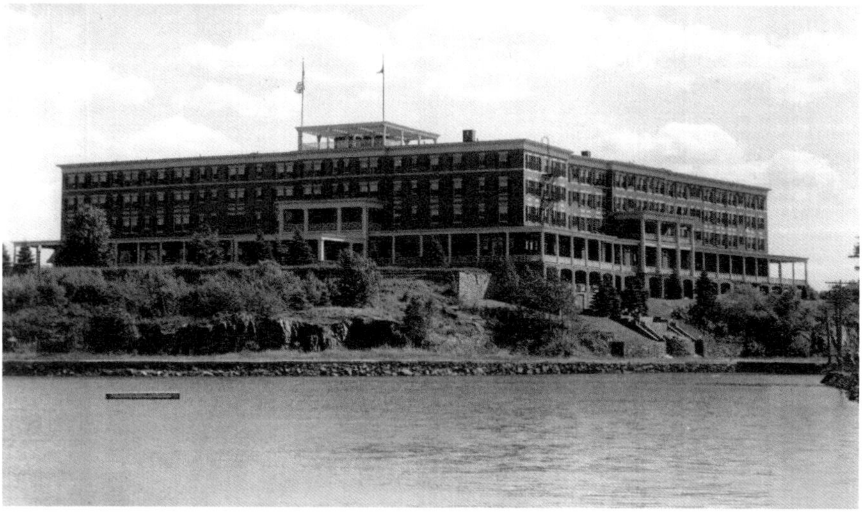

When the Marshall House burned down in January 1916, it was replaced with a four-story brick hotel, designed by noted architect John Calvin Stevens. In 1958, the Tufts family bought the resort. A group of year-round and summer residents purchased the property in 1971 and demolished the historic hotel. The Stage Neck Inn and condominiums now stand where the famous hotel once stood.

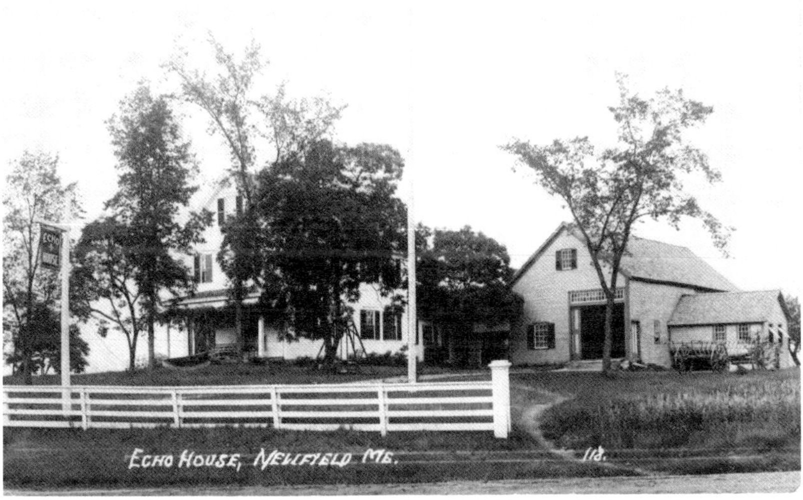

The Echo House in Newfield was built by Charles D. Staples, a house carpenter, in 1850. It was later owned by Orrin and Ruth Davis, and their daughter Dellie Lord and her husband Walter operated a boardinghouse known as the Echo House. Dell lived to be one hundred years old and stayed in the home with her son and his wife. The house burned down in 2003. *Courtesy of Newfield Historical Society.*

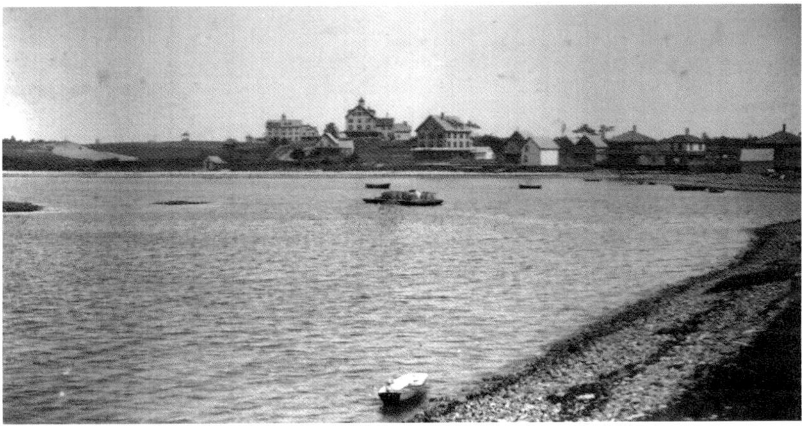

This circa 1895 view of Kennebunk Beach shows three hotels that once stood there and several of the early cottages. It's hard to imagine today as you drive around the Kennebunk Beach area that at one time there were at least eight large summer hotels there. There were also grocery stores, restaurants, a billiard hall and two bathhouses. The only hotels that remain are the Narragansett, now converted to condominiums, and the Seaside, although the original wooden hotel has been demolished. In this image, to the far left is the Wentworth House, first opened to guests during the Civil War. Across from that was the Eagle Rock Hotel; only the first floor remains and has been converted to a home. On the water, between the two mentioned hotels is Bay Cottage and an annex for the Sea View House, which stands to its right. Bay Cottage still stands, completely altered and enlarged. The Sea View was taken down in the 1960s.

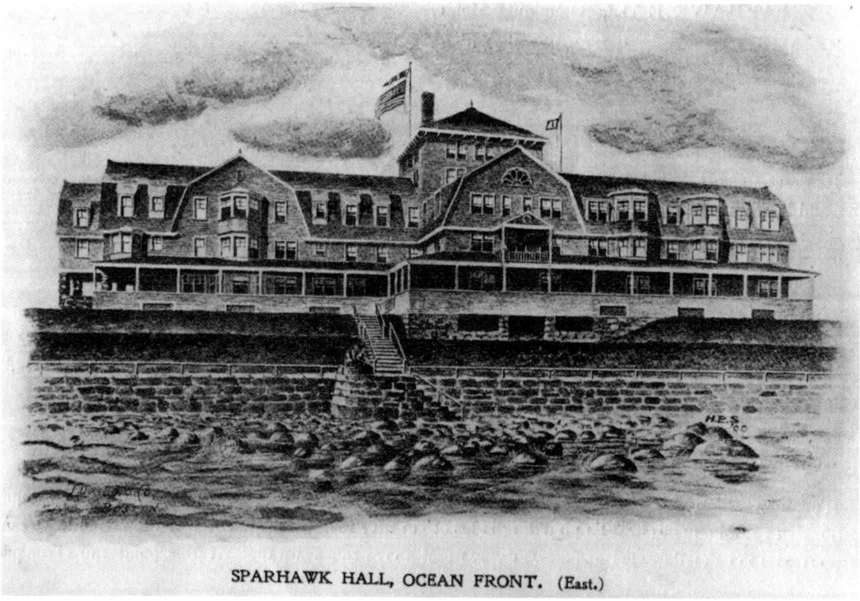

SPARHAWK HALL, OCEAN FRONT. (East.)

The Sparhawk Hotel in Ogunquit was owned and operated by Nehemiah P.M. Jacobs and was opened in 1897, but it burned down in October 1899. A new hotel, shown here, replaced it and opened in 1900. Jacobs died in 1931 and his daughter, Mary Kennedy, inherited the hotel. She sold it in 1955 to Mr. and Mrs. Walter Abbott. In 1963, Mr. and Mrs. Russell Ireland and Mr. and Mrs. Jules Voignier bought the hotel. They had it demolished and built a new motor court in its place. *Courtesy of Wells-Ogunquit Historical Society.*

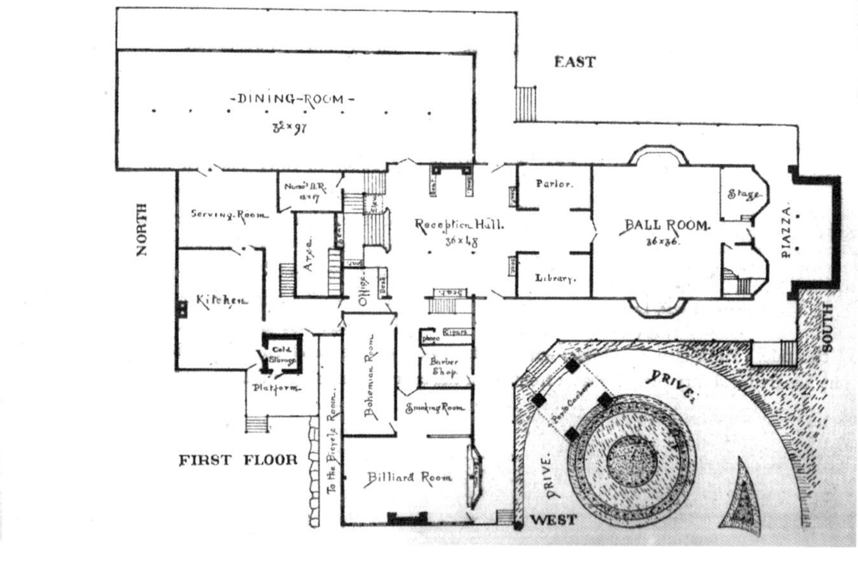

This is the first floor plan of the Sparhawk Hotel, showing the public rooms and common areas. *Courtesy of Wells-Ogunquit Historical Society.*

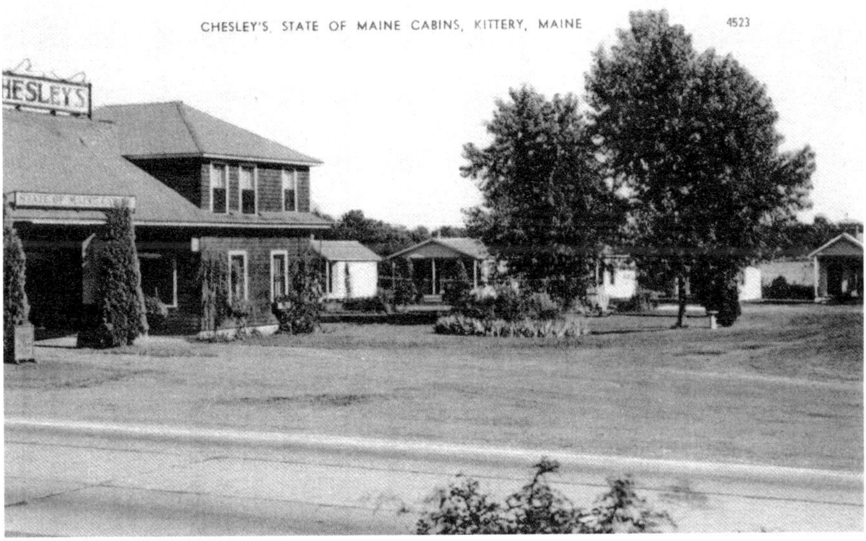

Chesley Cabins opened in 1929 when Arthur and Juliette Chesley added eight cabins behind their Kittery service station on Route 1. In 1963, the individual cabins were sold off, but the gas station remained and was used as an office. It was demolished for commercial development in June 1991.

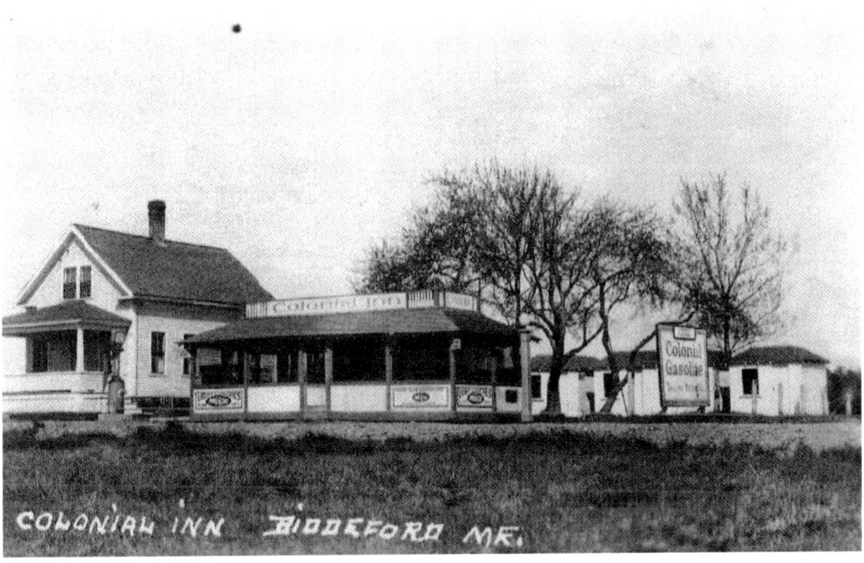

The Colonial Inn, circa 1925, was a gas station and diner that was located in Biddeford. The exact location is unknown and the house may still stand, but the diner and cabins are most likely gone.

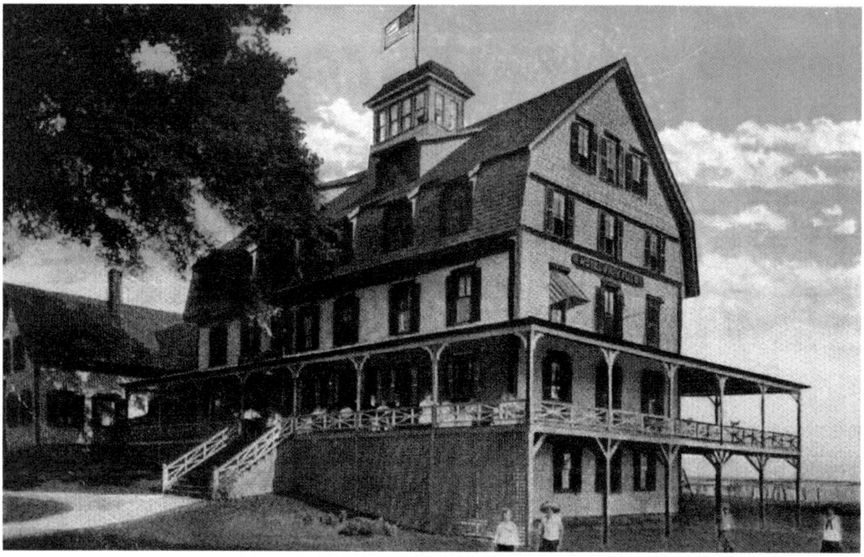

The Park Field Hotel was located at Kittery Point and was built in 1887 for Jesse E. Frisbee. It burned down in 1935.

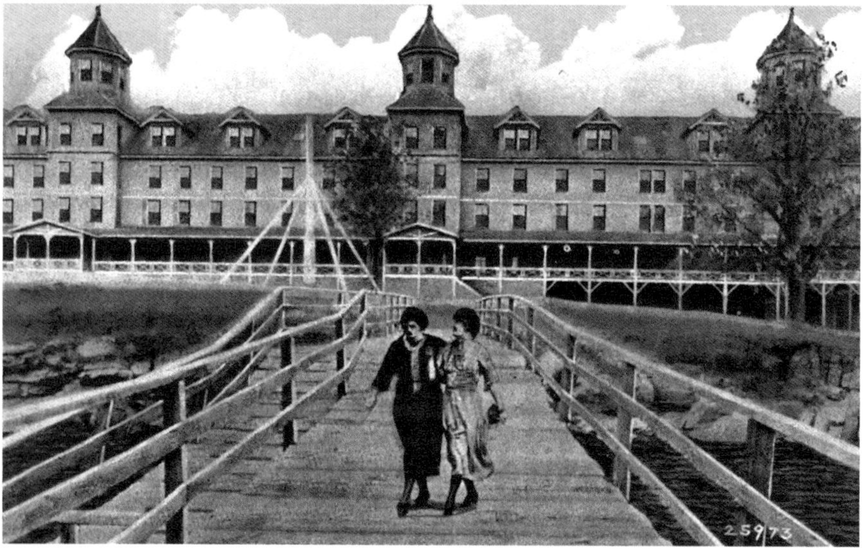

The Champernowne Hotel, in Kittery, was named after Captain Francis Champernowne, one of the first settlers to the area. The hotel was built by Horace Mitchell in 1890. John Mead Howells, a well-known architect, bought the hotel in 1920 and had it demolished. He used the land to expand his property and build a summer home for his son.

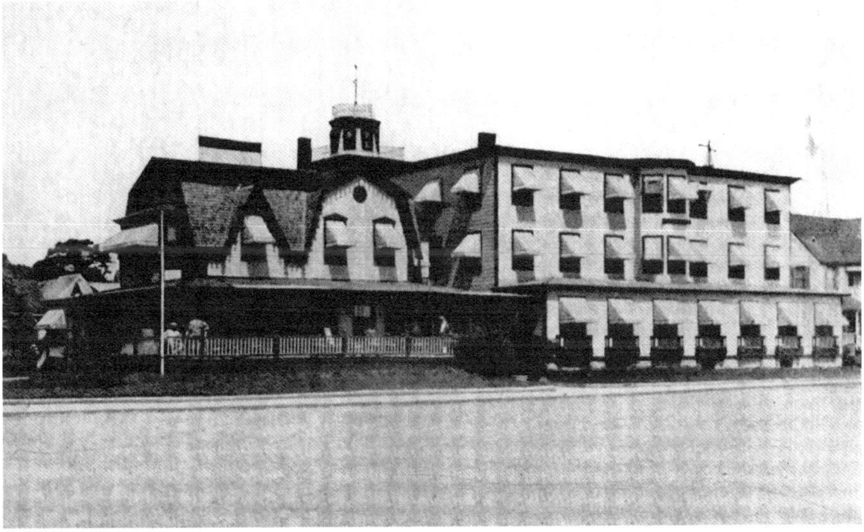

The Goodall Hotel was located between Bay Avenue and Pearl Street in Old Orchard Beach and started out as the summer "cottage" of Sanford mill owner Thomas Goodall. In 1919, Nelson McKenney bought the cottage and turned it into a summer hotel by removing the rear portion of the cottage and adding on more rooms. In 1946, the hotel name was changed to the Gables and it remained in business until 1982, when it was torn down.

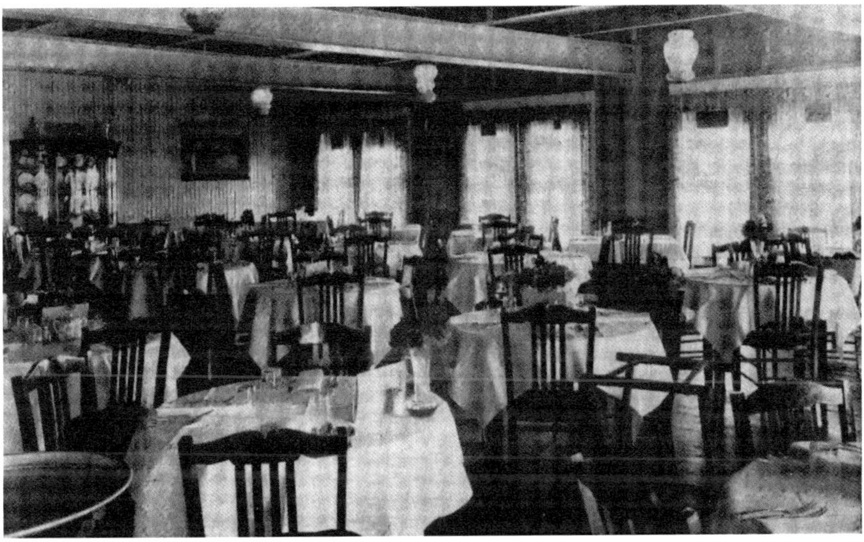

Shown here is the dining room of the Goodall Hotel.

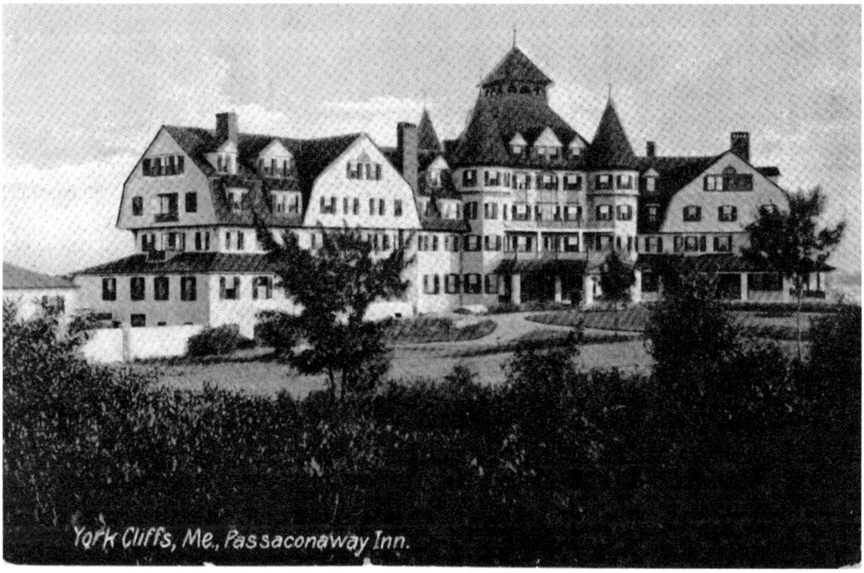

The Passaconaway Inn, in York, was built in 1892 by architect Edward Blaisdell. The inn was completed in just over forty days and was part of a resort development called York Cliffs. It fell victim to the changing times following World War I that included new tax laws and the Depression. It was demolished in 1937.

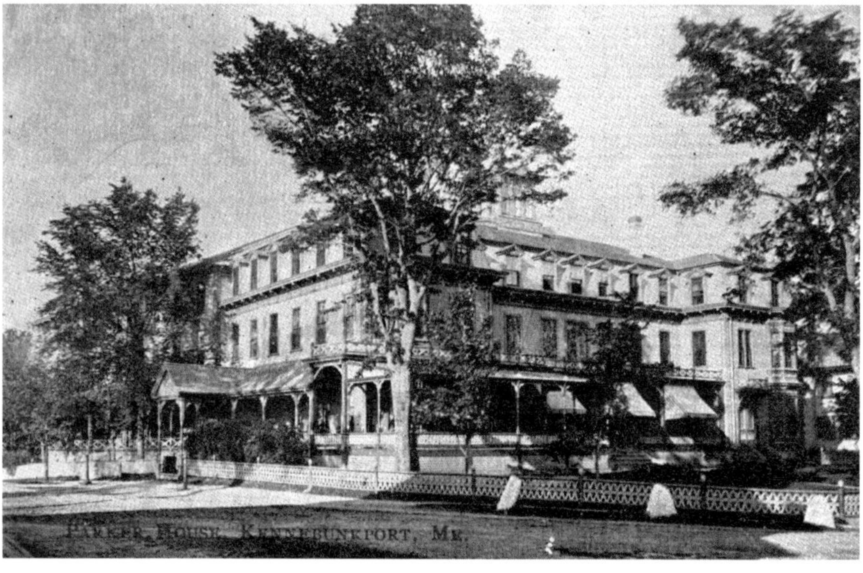

The Parker House, built in 1877, stood on Temple Street in Kennebunkport, where the post office is now located. Mr. Parker owned and operated the hotel, but it was never popular with summer visitors because it wasn't located on the beach. Because of this it went through several owners and managers. It was demolished in 1940 and replaced with the post office. *Courtesy of Greg Hubbard.*

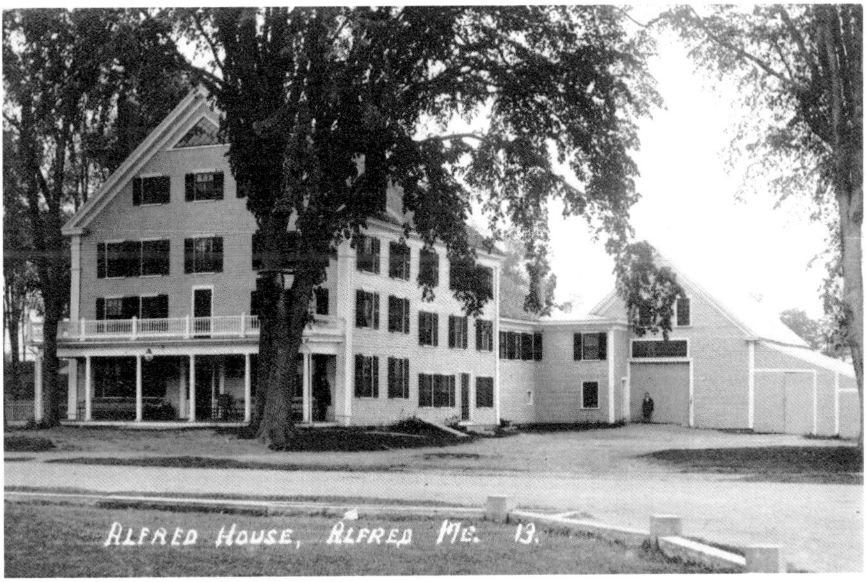

The original section of the Alfred House, in Alfred, was built in 1807 by William Parsons. General Samuel Leighton purchased the building in 1832 and added the four-story section seen here. It was a busy inn through the nineteenth century, housing and feeding travelers and accommodating lawyers, judges and others who had business to conduct at the county courthouse. It was demolished in the 1930s.

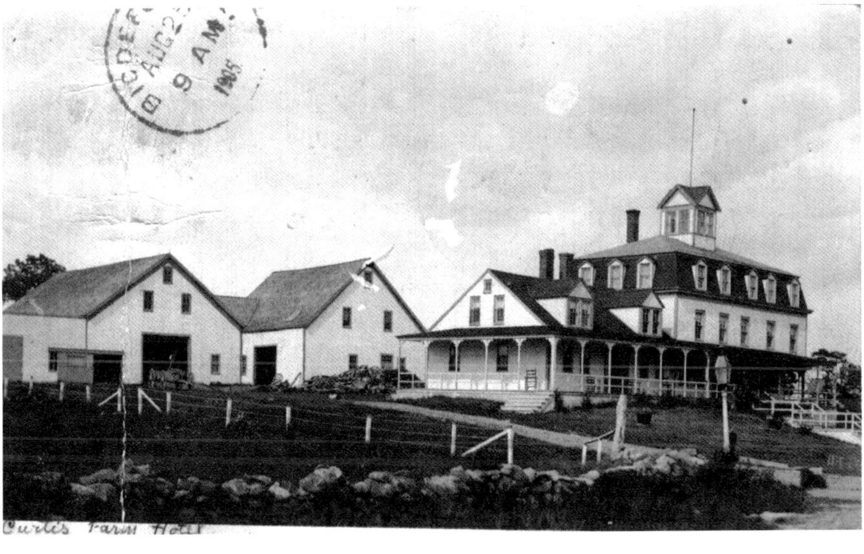

The Curtis Farm Hotel was located at Fortune's Rock and appears to have been an older farmhouse that had a large, three-story addition added to it to accommodate summer guests. It was probably lost in the October 1917 fire.

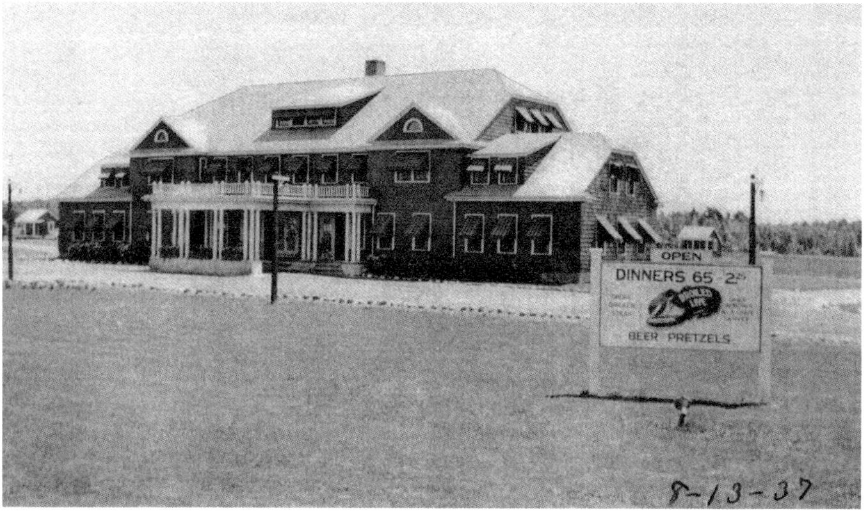

The Cascade Inn and Cabins was built near the Saco-Scarborough line in 1929. It was built to accommodate the tourists who flocked to Maine by car each summer. The Cascade Inn was one of the most popular restaurants in southern Maine for tourists as well as locals. Hundreds of wedding receptions and events were held there between 1930 and 1980.

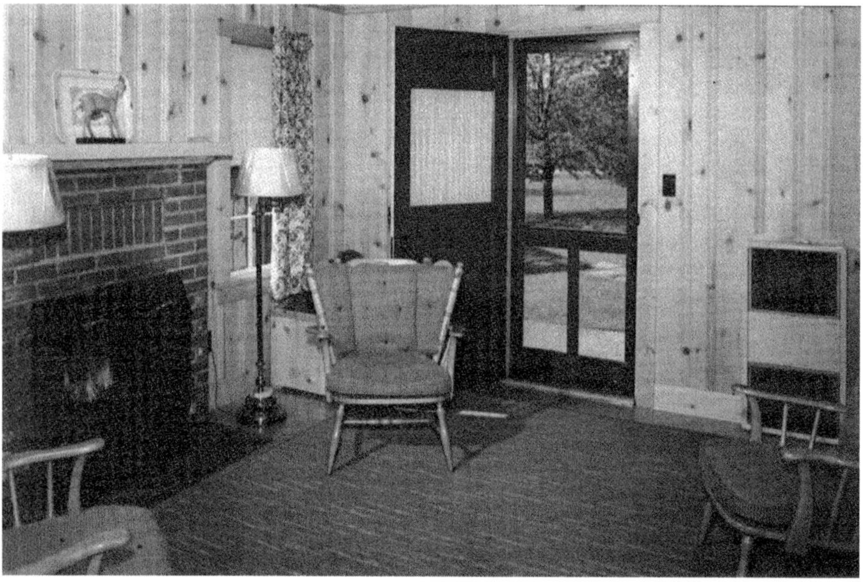

The interior of one of the cabins. Each cabin featured a fireplace, knotty pine walls and maple furniture. The main building and cabins all had yellow roofs, and the complex was laid out in a diamond shape with cabins alongside the driveways and neatly kept grounds. Elliot Chamberlain destroyed this Route 1 landmark for condominiums and commercial development in 2008. Many of the cabins were sold and moved away.

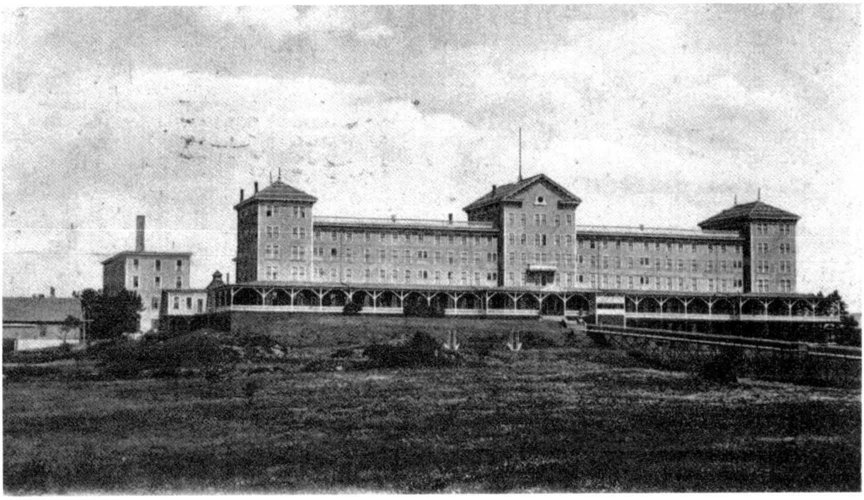

The Old Orchard House stood near St. Margaret's Church on Saco Avenue, in Old Orchard Beach. It was built in 1876 and replaced a hotel that had burned down the year before. This large hotel could accommodate five hundred guests, and it was one of the premier hotels in Old Orchard Beach. The Staples family operated the hotel until 1922. It was torn down in 1943.

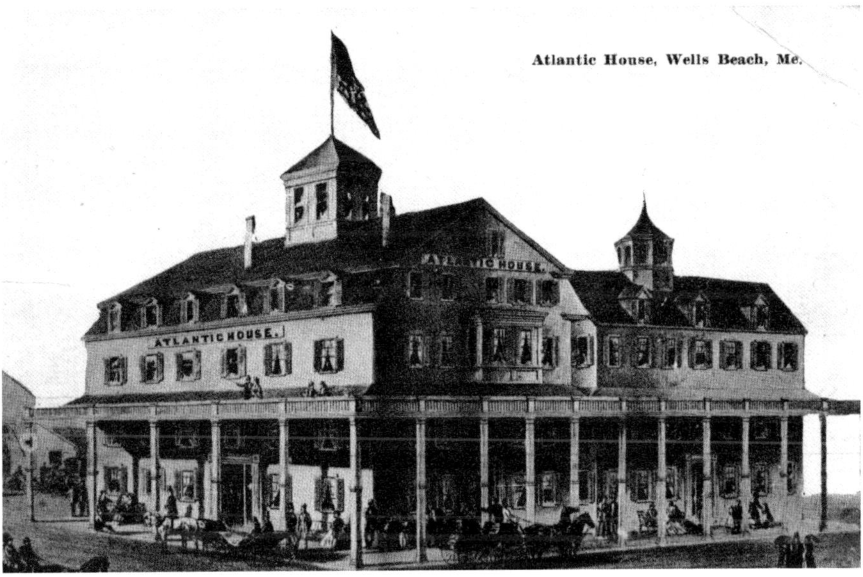

The Atlantic House was the first hotel to be built at Wells Beach and was constructed circa 1850. It was a large wooden building that offered guests a bowling alley, tennis courts and a steam laundry. It burned down on November 13, 1885.

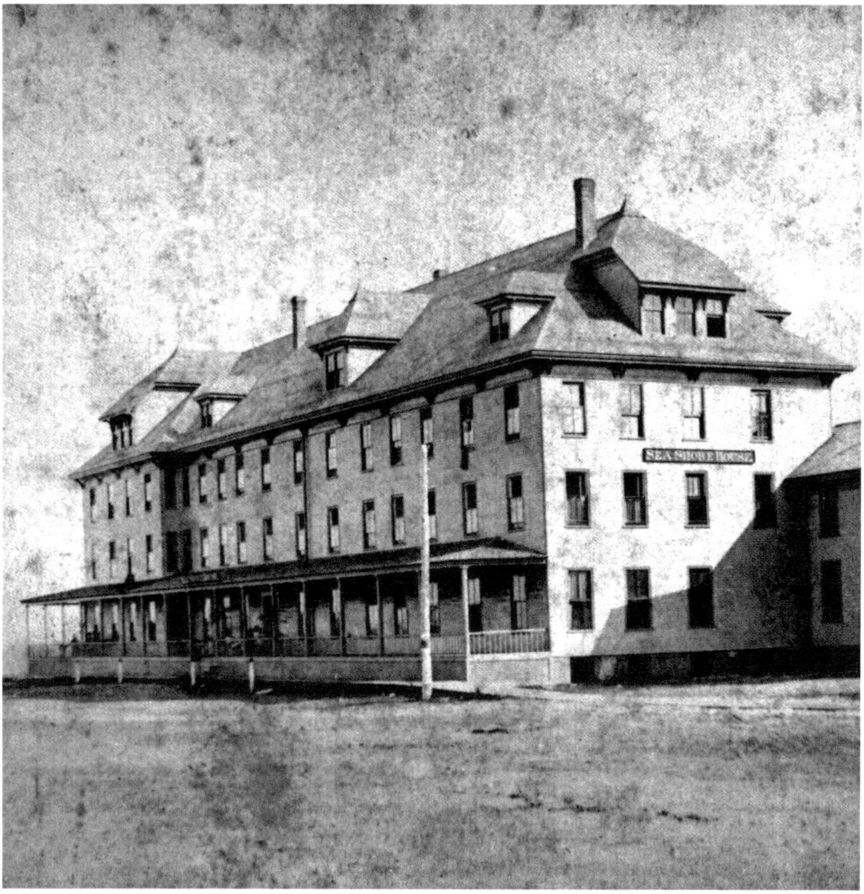

The Sea Shore House, built in 1873, was one of the first hotels in Old Orchard. This image dates to circa 1885, and the hotel was located where Palace Play Land now stands. The Sea Shore could accommodate three hundred guests and was owned and managed by Frank Staples. The contractor was George H. Herring, and he also built the railroad station in Old Orchard and many other buildings in the area. The Sea Shore House was one of the hotels lost in the Old Orchard Beach fire on August 15, 1907. This fire burned over seventy-five acres and destroyed all but one hotel. It was the worst fire in Old Orchard's history. Seventeen hotels and nearly one hundred homes and cottages were destroyed by the fire, which was believed to have been caused by a female employee of the Emerson House who was heating tongs to curl her hair and somehow knocked over the oil lamp. There wasn't much that could be done to stop the fire, considering the inadequate equipment of the times, the lack of water pressure and the often cheaply built, wooden and ornate Victorian hotels and cottages that lined the streets of Old Orchard Beach. It's interesting to note that at the time of the fire a report in the *New York Times* was headlined: "Fire Merely Hastened Old Orchard's Doom; Its Decline Began Ten Years Ago with Advent of Trolley Cars and Cheap Excursion Trains." The *Times* felt then that the glory days of Old Orchard were over and the famous summer resort would never be rebuilt. This outlook was wrong. The area was rebuilt, but the new Old Orchard Beach was very different from what it had been before the fire and would attract the working class, consisting of those who used the trains and trolleys mentioned in the *Times* article.

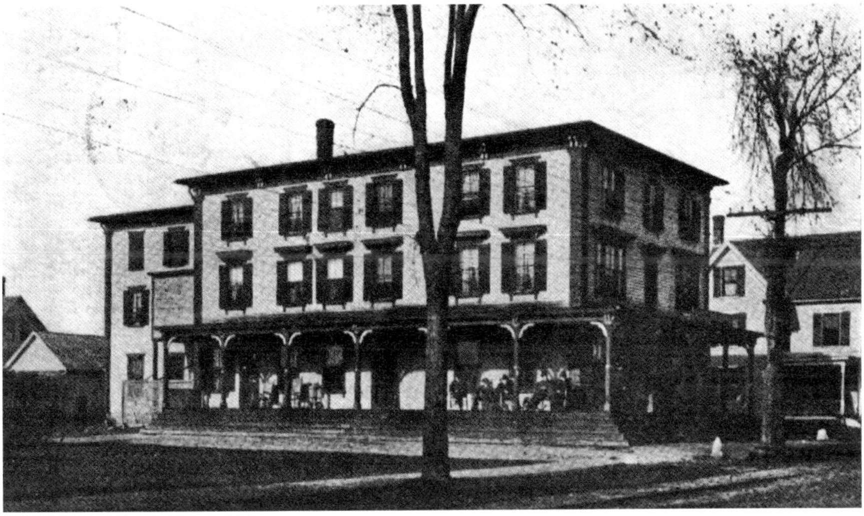

The Hotel Sanford stood where T.D. Bank is located today on Main Street. It was originally called the Allen House and was built in 1888. Willard Hanson Bennett started working there in 1895 and ran the hotel for twenty-four years. It was demolished in 1934.

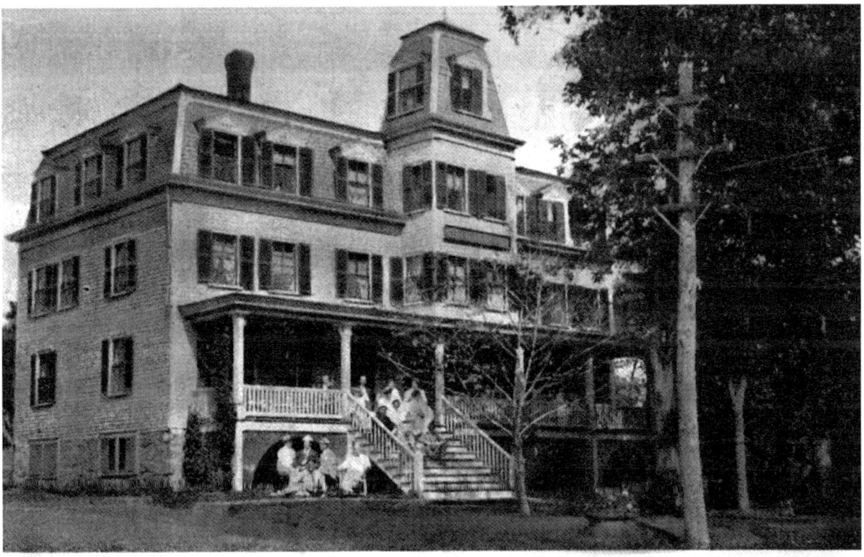

The Rockland, Ogunquit, Maine

The Maxwell House was located on Main Street in Ogunquit, where Key Bank now stands. It was built by Barack Maxwell in 1765 and served as a stage stop along the Post Road. Warren and Arthur Maxwell were the last family members to operate the inn, selling in 1902. The mansard roof, tower and front porch were later alterations to the original building. It burned on August 14, 1968. *Courtesy of Wells-Ogunquit Historical Society.*

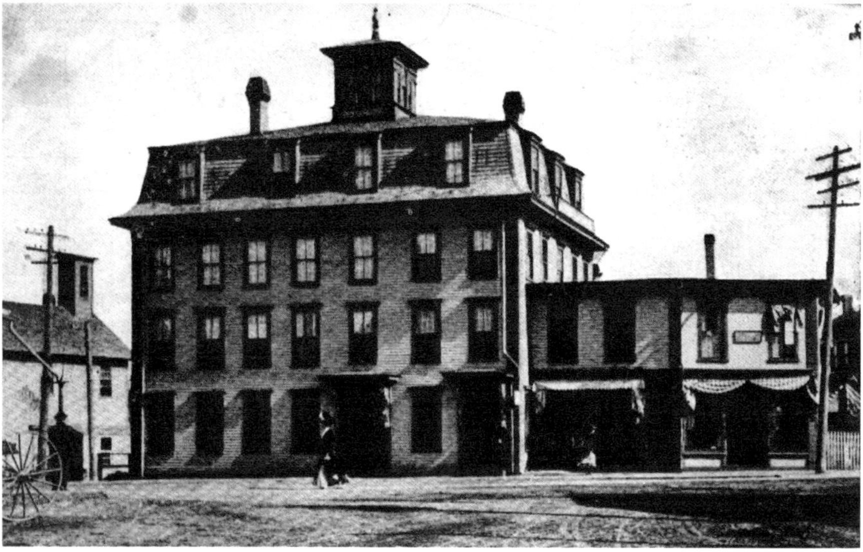

The Grant House stood opposite Sullivan Square in Berwick and was a popular hotel at the turn of the last century. It was demolished before 1940, and a gas station now occupies the site. *Courtesy of Brian Cincotta.*

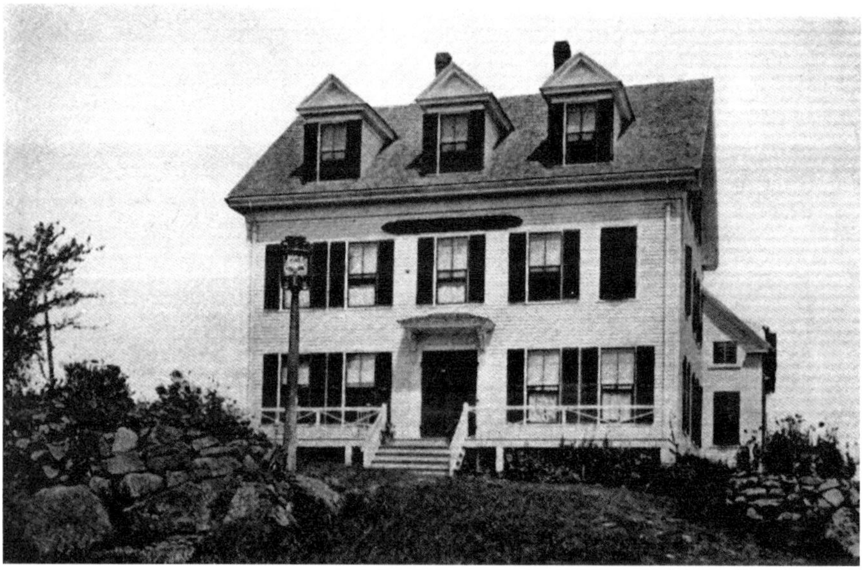

Luther Emerson bought this property in Cape Porpoise in 1905 and added the front section seen here to an existing home on the site. He opened it as a hotel named the Prospect House. He sold the business in 1910 and it burned on January 16, 1913. *Courtesy of Greg Hubbard.*

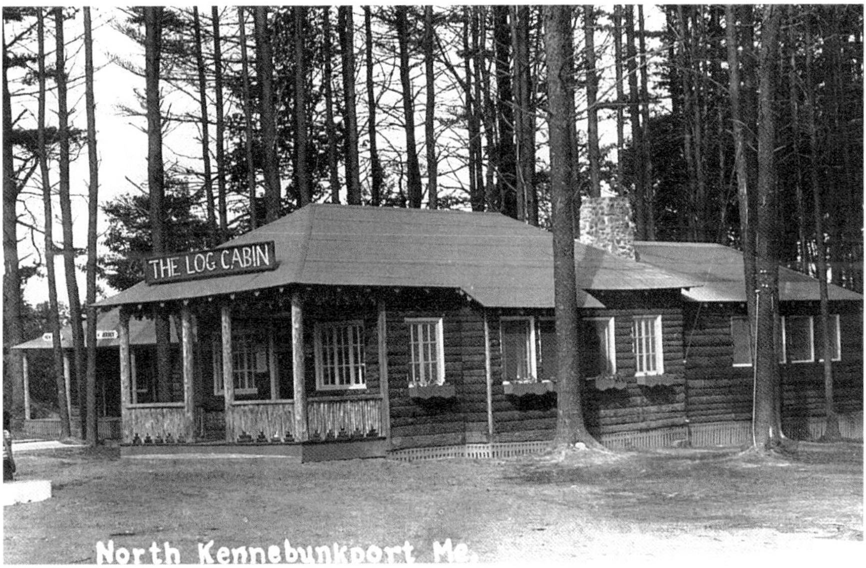

The Log Cabin Motor Court on Route 1, in Arundel, was opened in 1932 by Edward and Esther Tibbets and was located where USA Antiques is today. Each cottage was designed to look like a small log cabin and each cabin was named for a state. After the business closed in the 1970s, some of the cabins were sold off and the rest were demolished.

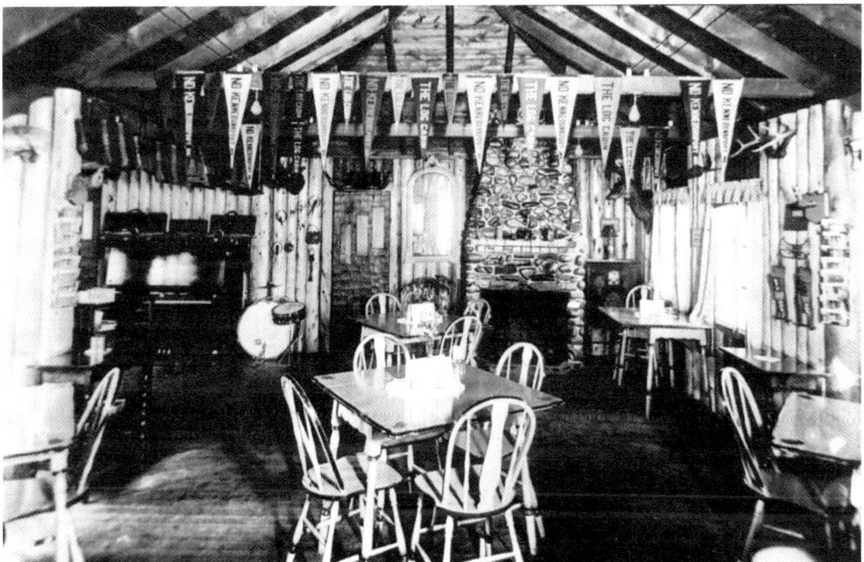

The Log Cabin Ballroom was part of the Log Cabin Motor Court complex and was a popular place in the 1940s and 1950s for locals to gather. This image shows the inside of the dance hall probably circa 1940. In January 1964, the ballroom burned down and was not rebuilt.

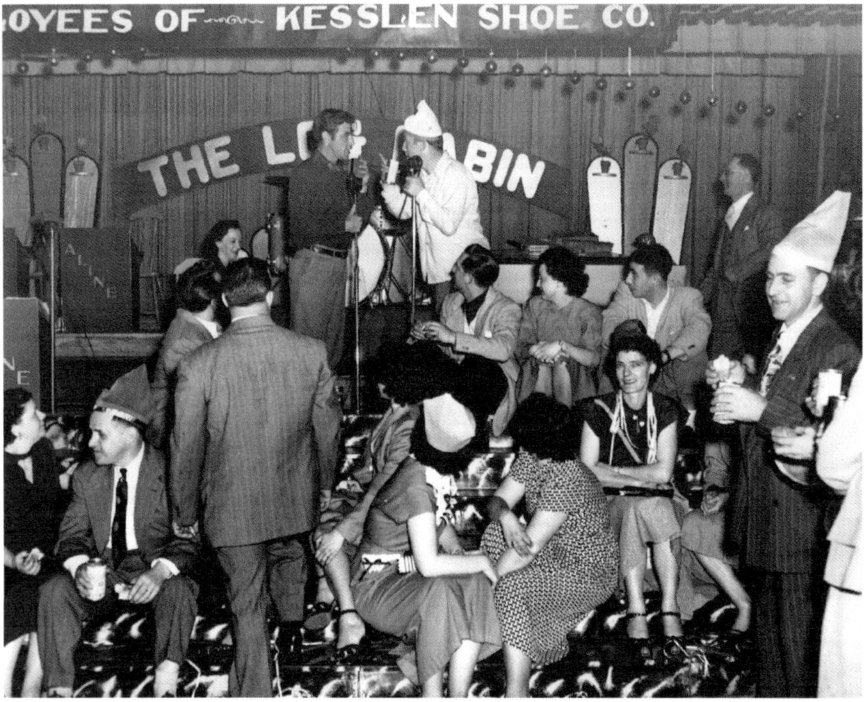

This photograph shows Kesslen Shoe Company employees, circa 1950, celebrating at the Log Cabin Ballroom. It could be a Christmas or New Year's party. Kesslen Shoe was located in Kennebunk and operated until 1978.

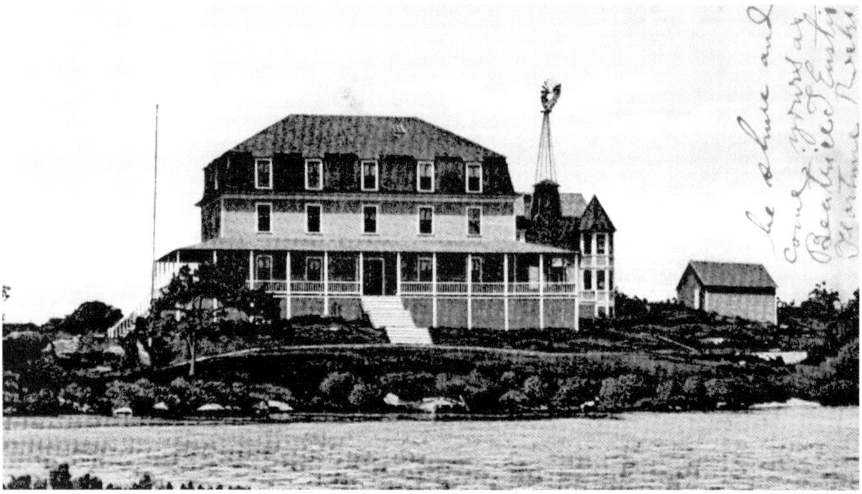

The Hotel Rox, built in 1909, stood at Fortune's Rock, which is part of Biddeford, Maine. It burned down on January 14, 1915, but was rebuilt. The new hotel burned down in the 1947 fire.

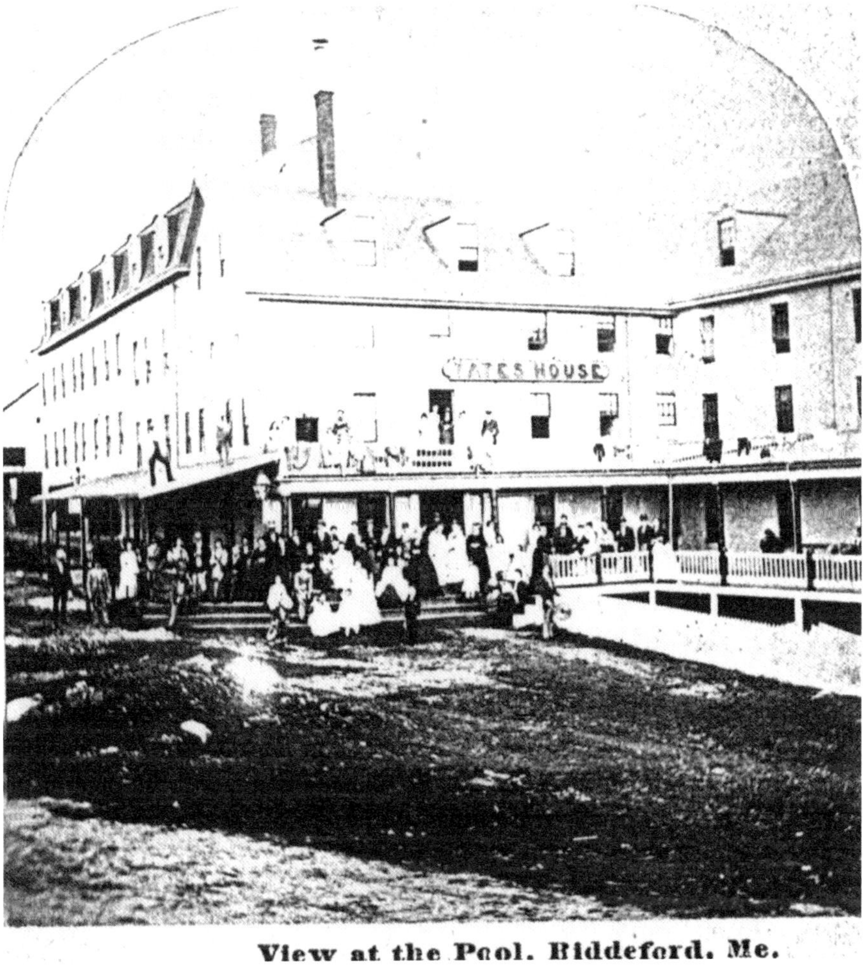

The Yates House was located at Biddeford Pool and had several owners and different names starting in 1844. It was originally a private home that was turned into a summer hotel. Fred Yates bought the hotel sometime before 1879 and changed the name to the Yates House. It was destroyed on June 15, 1884, in a fire that burned five other nearby buildings. *Courtesy of McArthur Library.*

CHAPTER THREE

SUMMER BUSINESSES

At the turn of the last century, summer visitors spent more time outside at the seashore, canoeing, picnicking, bike riding or touring the area in horse-drawn wagons. Before air conditioning, or even electric fans, the large hotels would get awfully uncomfortable in the summer heat, and the large hotel kitchens with wood- or coal-burning stoves didn't help either. Unlike today's visitors who arrive in air-conditioned cars, dine in air-conditioned restaurants and sleep in air-conditioned hotels, the early tourists to York County really had to rough it. The early hotels were built as close to the shore as possible and offered wraparound porches to catch the cool ocean air. Inland hotels were built along the many ponds and lakes of the county, which also provided recreation and cool breezes. Uncomfortable and restraining bathing suits allowed men and women the opportunity to cool off in the ocean or lakes, and picnics along the shore and rivers were also popular.

The large hotels all had dining rooms for their guests, and unlike today's summertime fare, they served full-course dinners of fried chicken and steaks along with seafood. Other courses included fruit, cheese, salads, ice cream and other desserts like blueberry pie. Clambakes were special events and allowed guests to dine outside. But inside, proper dress was required.

At the beginning of the twentieth century, tearooms became popular. These small establishments were usually operated and staffed by women. At that time, women did not dine alone or in groups in public restaurants, unless escorted by a man. The early tearooms changed that by giving women a place to dine out unescorted. The Whistling Oyster in Ogunquit opened in 1907, and a tearoom existed in Fortune's Rock at about the same time. The Grist Mill Restaurant in Kennebunkport started as a tearoom, first opened in 1940. The Salmon Falls Library, on Route 202 in Hollis, originally opened as a tearoom and library. By the 1920s, tearooms had opened in most York County towns, especially those that attracted tourists. Former barns, blacksmith shops, fishing shacks, gristmills and old homes were converted to tearooms, and in addition to a light lunch and afternoon tea, they sold candy, gifts and antiques. The Whistling Oyster had a Christmas shop that was popular with visitors. Libby's Tea Room on the Kennebunk and Wells town line (still standing but derelict) offered luncheon and tea along with fine antiques for sale, as did Tuck's Antiques in Kennebunkport.

Another popular attraction was the casinos that were built along the coast. Not like the gambling casinos that we know today, these early casinos were places to dine and dance. They offered shore dinners to customers in large dining rooms and wide verandas to stroll on after dinner. In Old Orchard Beach, the casino was located at the end of an eighteen-hundred-foot pier to capture the cooler ocean air. York and Ogunquit both had casinos, as did Wells, which also included an ice cream parlor. The Cape Porpoise casino was located at the end of the trolley line and another casino operated at Old Falls, in Kennebunk, at the other end of the line.

In Old Orchard Beach, the Sea Side Park, one of the first amusement parks in the area, opened in 1902. It was built on twenty-five acres overlooking the beach and ocean. It contributed to Old Orchard's change from a genteel summer resort to a rollicking summertime town of amusement parks and souvenir shops. With the opening of the trolley line, millworkers from Biddeford and Saco could visit on the weekends and then return home at night.

This chapter also includes images from Camp Mo-Mo-Da-Yo, once located in Limington and first opened in 1907. This girls' camp operated until the late 1960s. Another girls' camp was located on Ossipee Lake in Waterboro. Boys' and girls' camps of the early twentieth century appealed to urban youths for their exposure to nature and the simple life. These camps focused on developing skills, sports, loyalty and camp spirit. By 1940, forty-one all-summer camps for girls were in operation in the state, many in the northeast. In York County, in addition to the camps mentioned above, there was Lanier Camp in Eliot, which operated from 1908 to 1940, and Rosemary Cottage, also in Eliot and founded in the 1880s.

York County, Maine, has been the location for some of the state's best restaurants, many of which used to operate seasonally. Many of these restaurants are now closed but are fondly remembered today. They include the Dan Sing Fan and the Whistling Oyster, both in Ogunquit; the Grist

Mill, Kennebunkport; Spiller's Restaurant, Cape Neddick; and the Glen Mor Restaurant, Route 1 in Kennebunk. The Glen Mor, like the others, was family owned and operated and was well known for its baked goods. It was a "must stop" for tourists every year. It stood across from another summertime favorite, the Kennebunk Drive-In. Unfortunately, I couldn't locate an image of the Kennebunk Drive-In or the Saco Drive-In to include in this chapter. The Kennebunk Drive-In opened in 1951 and was designed by H.J. McKenny of the Theater Supply Company in Boston. It closed for good in 1981. The Saco Drive-In, the second-oldest running drive-in in the country, still operates each summer but may become another lost landmark soon if much-needed repairs are not made. It once had a fountain featuring Bambi and other characters from that movie cast in concrete that could be seen along the edge of the front entrance. It was opened by Eugene V. Boragine in 1939 and originally featured a snack bar, playground and a dance floor, all gone now. There was also the Kittery-York Drive-In on Route 1 in Kittery, and drive-ins in Cornish and Acton as well. All of these were popular evening activities for visiting families after spending the day at the beach. It was fun, although much of the evening was spent swatting mosquitoes!

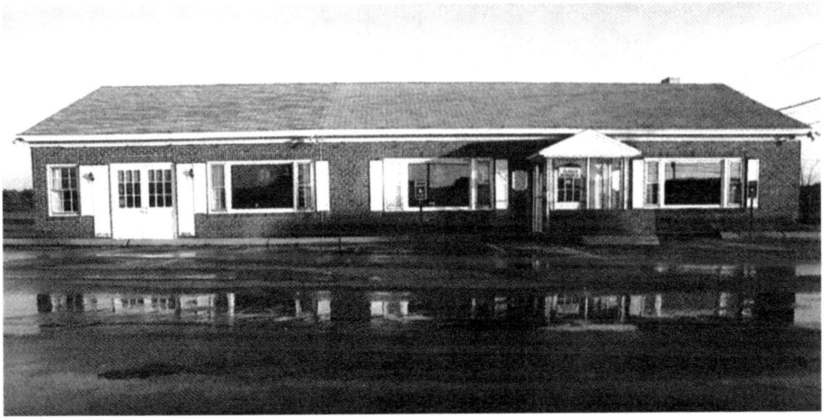

The Glen Mor Restaurant stood on Portland Road, in Kennebunk, where Talbot's clothing store is now located. It was opened in June 1963 by Chet and Majorie Eaton. It quickly became popular with locals and tourists alike and was famous for its pastries and baked goods, which my grandmother, Gertrude Barrett Hutchins, made daily for almost twenty years. An arson fire leveled the landmark on December 14, 1997, but people still talk about the restaurant today.

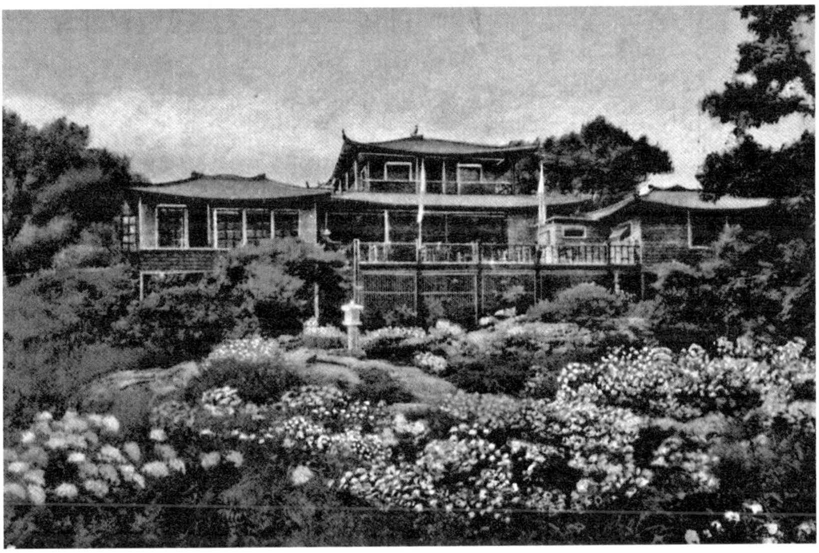

The Dan Sing Fan Tea Room stood on Shore Road in Ogunquit and was built to resemble a Japanese pagoda. The date of construction is unknown. Paul Coolidge bought the property in 1920, and the tearoom was built circa 1925 by him or his son Richard. Richard's adopted son, Osavaldo, took over the restaurant in 1964. He was born in Genoa, Italy, and wrestled for Italy in the 1948 Olympics in London. Osavaldo divided his time between his native Italy and Ogunquit and ran an Italian restaurant out of the building. It was sold in 1995 to Richard and Marjorie Lion, who had the building burned for fire practice so that they could build a not-so-attractive home on the property.

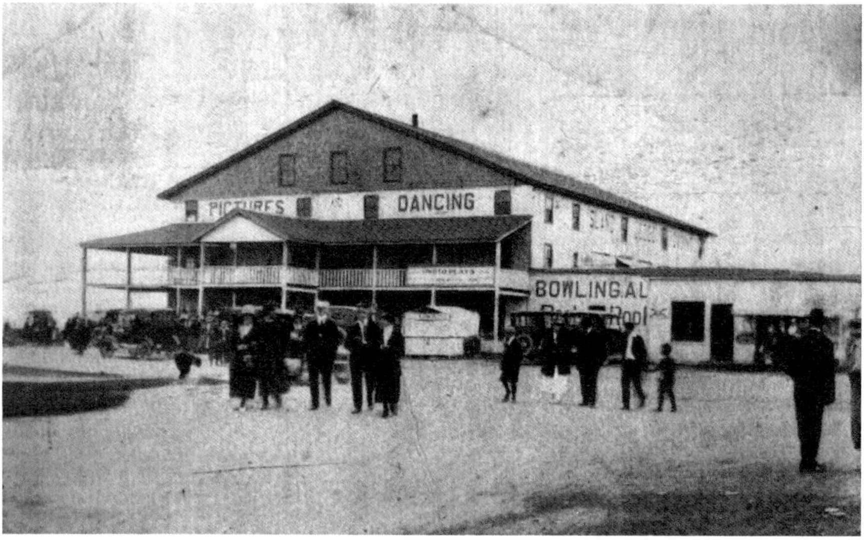

The Island Ledge Casino at Wells Beach was located on the ocean near today's Forbe's Restaurant. John Davis bought the property in 1913 and built a casino, which he sold to Island Ledge Casino in 1920. Today the building has been made over into condominiums and shops and very little remains of the original building.

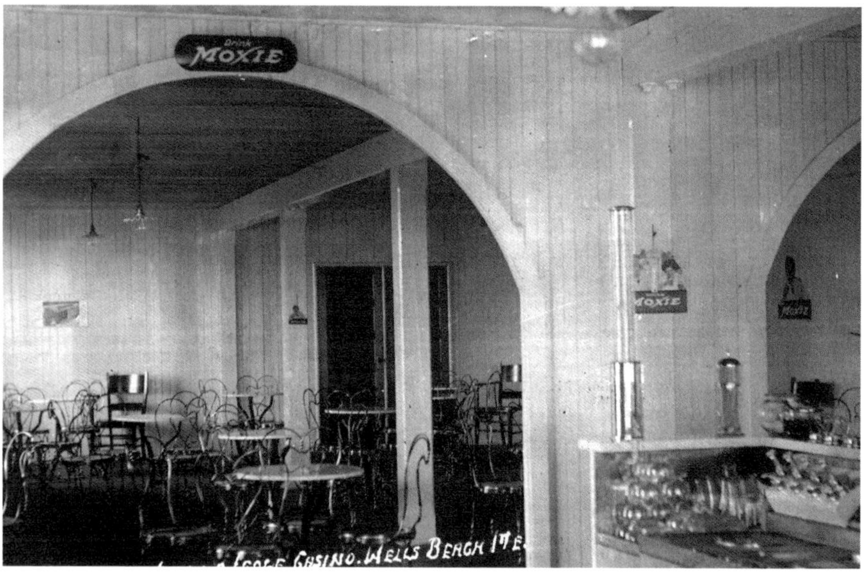

The Island Ledge Casino ice cream parlor. *Courtesy of Wells-Ogunquit Historical Society.*

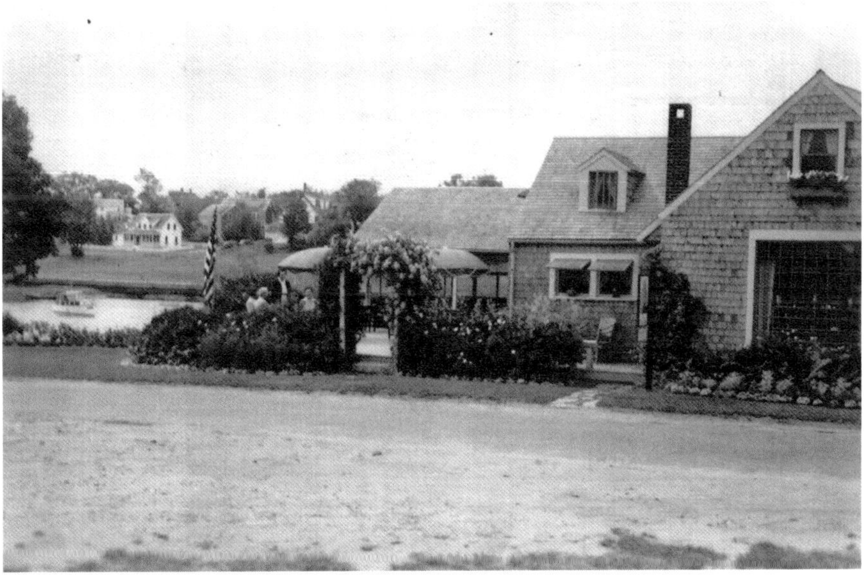

Tearooms were popular in America during the first half of the twentieth century and were the only places where women could eat out and meet their friends. Restaurants then were reserved for men only, and no single women would ever think about going into one alone. Most tearooms included gift shops and were largely run by women who hired other women as cooks and waitresses. In 1907, Phoebe Scott rented a one-room shack at Perkins Cove, Ogunquit, and opened a tearoom called the Whistling Oyster. The unusual name came from a story originally published in *Punch* magazine about a London innkeeper who discovered a whistling oyster in his kitchen in 1843. This amazing oyster could whistle actual tunes, according to the story.

Helen E. Ryan and Joy Hawley bought the tearoom in 1929, along with the house that stood next to the restaurant, which was considered the oldest house in Ogunquit. Ryan and Hawley opened a gift shop in the house that offered Christmas items and fine gifts. After the season was over, they moved to Florida, where they ran two exclusive gift shops under the Whistling Oyster name.

John Parella and Mary Kennedy bought the restaurant in 1964 and turned the small tearoom into an upscale restaurant that was the social center of the resort town every summer. Margaret Hamilton, who had played the wicked witch in *The Wizard of Oz*, read Christmas stories to children each year, a popular event. The actors who appeared at the Ogunquit Play House were frequent customers, especially after performances. The Whistling Oyster burned down in August 1976 but was rebuilt and reopened on April 30, 1977. Mary Kennedy died in 1981 and Parella sold the building, but not the name, in 1987. He died in 1991.

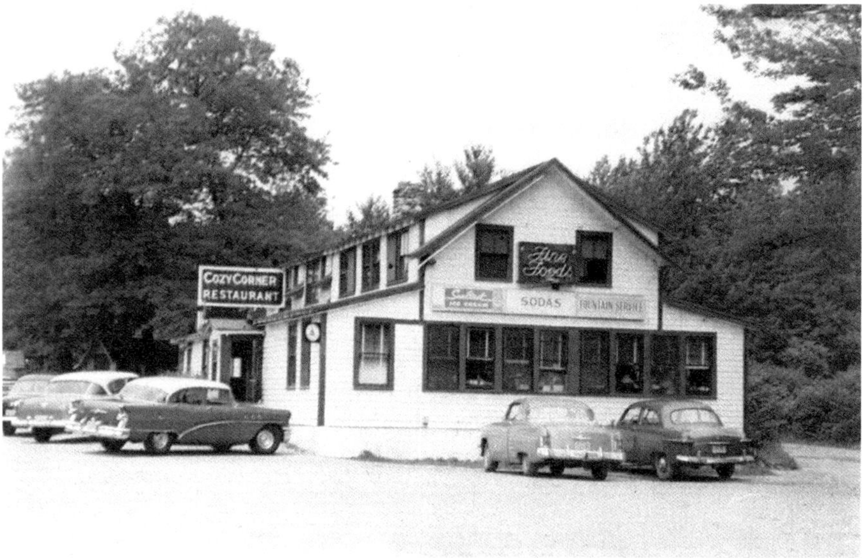

The Cozy Corner Restaurant was located by the railroad bridge in Wells near the Kennebunk line. Before Route 1 was straightened in 1978, it ran off to the left side of this picture, and Route 9, out of sight, veered off to the right. Mary Capell bought the land from Elmer J. Cole and Albert H. Smith in 1910. Capell's obituary stated that she had established one of the first eating places on Route 1 between Boston and Portland. Customers referred to owner Mary as "Mother Capell" and "Mother Capell of the iron Bridge." She lived above the restaurant. Her parents, Daniel and Arvilla Swan, had once managed the Mousam House in Kennebunk. Capell sold the business in 1930 to Addie Watson and held the mortgage. She then moved to a boardinghouse in Wells. Watson sold the business back to Capell in 1932, and Capell continued to operate the restaurant until her death in February 1941. Sometime between 1941 and 1947, under different owners, the place was raided for illegal gambling machines, something many roadside establishments turned to in order to bring in extra money as business slowed during the war. FBI agents arrived in an unmarked train car, which stopped on the bridge next to the restaurant. Then they jumped out, surprising the owner and customers. Howard and Lillian True owned and operated the restaurant from 1947 to 1962, apparently keeping things on the up and up. Before being demolished in October 1968, the place had been used as an antiques shop. Today, Route 1 runs right through where the popular restaurant once stood.

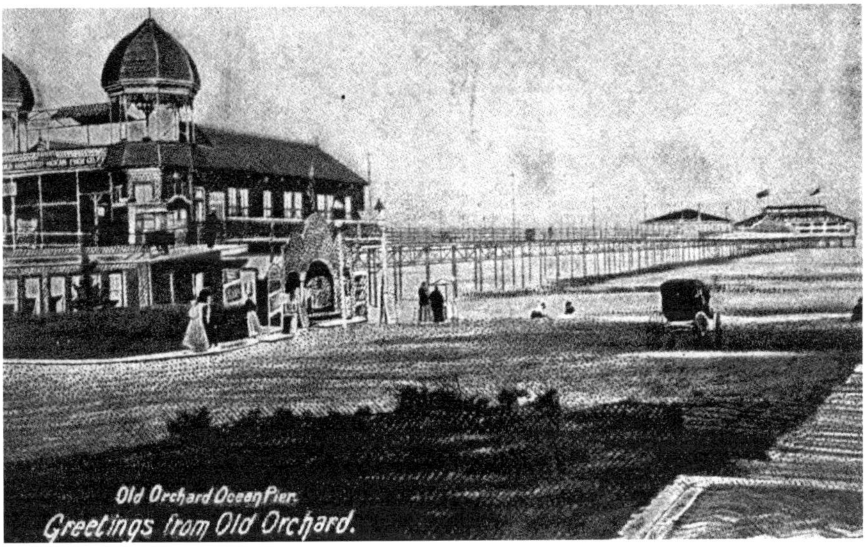

The Old Orchard Pier, circa 1900, was first opened on July 2, 1898, and was 1,800 feet long with a casino at the end. The original entrance, shown here, burned down in 1907. A storm in 1909 destroyed the casino and 300 feet of the pier. The casino was rebuilt on a shortened pier. The pier was destroyed in the winter storm of February 1978 and was rebuilt.

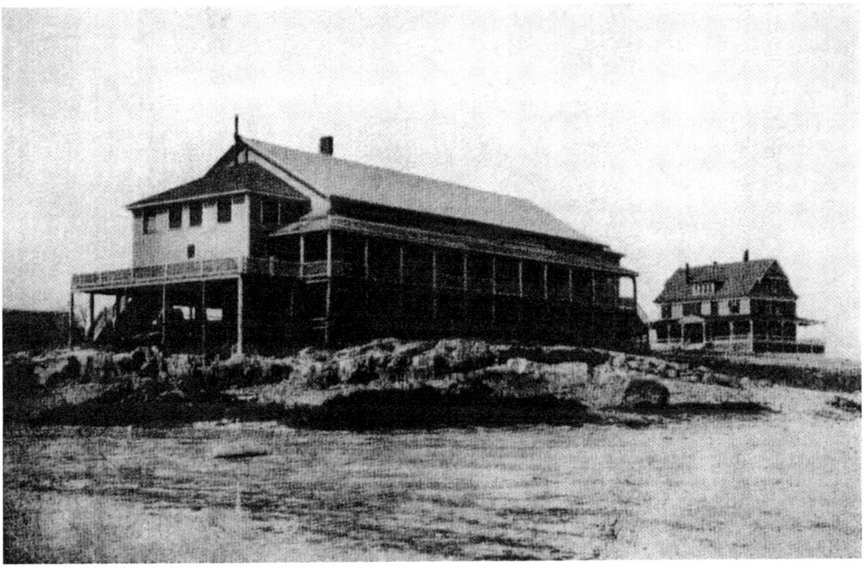

The Cape Porpoise Casino stood on Bickford's Island and marked the end of the trolley line from Sanford (it later became part of the Atlantic Shore Line). It was built in 1900 and featured a restaurant, wide porches and a dance floor. It burned down in September 1915.

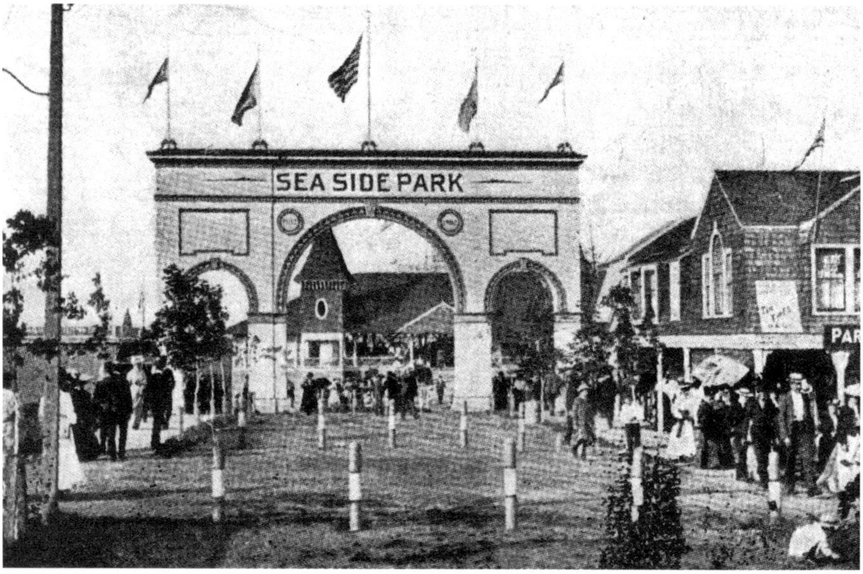

Sea Side Park, at Old Orchard Beach, was billed as the "Coney Island of the East" and opened in 1902. The arch, designed by John Calvin Stevens, was fifty feet wide and thirty feet high and topped with electric lights. This was the Imperial Street entrance and the ticket office, on the left, still stands today as the Imperial Waters Motel. Seaside Park was partially destroyed by the August 15, 1907 fire and was rebuilt, but it closed for good by 1924.

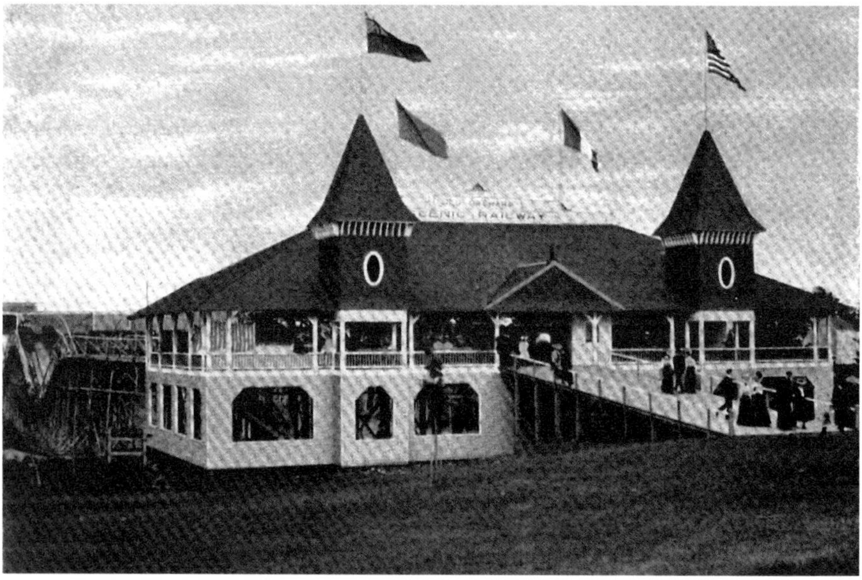

The scenic railway at Sea Side Park, early 1900s.

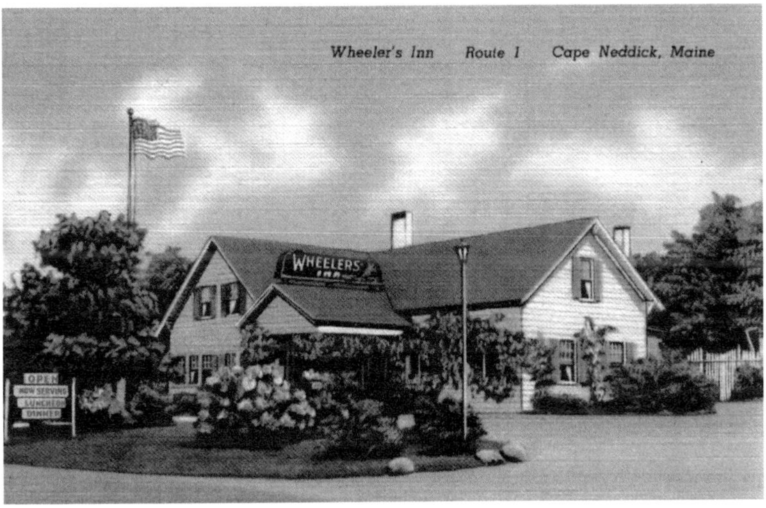

In 1926, Octavius and Velma Tapley opened the Triangle Lunch in Cape Neddick on this site. It was named for the shape of the property, which was located at the intersection of Routes 1 and 1-A. In 1929, Alpheus and Nina Spiller bought the business and reopened it as Spiller's Inn. When the Spillers relocated to York Beach, the restaurant was sold and the name changed to Wheeler's Inn. It became the Cape Neddick Inn in the early 1970s when Peter Camplin bought it. It burned down on May 9, 1985, and a new building resembling the old restaurant was built on the site.

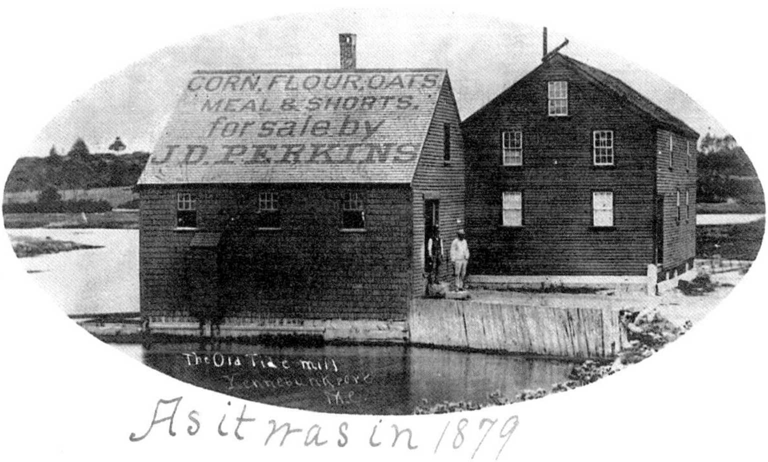

The Grist Mill Restaurant, in Kennebunkport, started out as a tidal mill built in 1740 by Tristam Perkins that remained in operation until 1939. Louise Lombard, a Perkins descendant, and her husband Arthur opened the mill as a summer restaurant in 1940. The historic building, which was on the National Register of Historic Places, burned down on September 14, 1994. It had no sprinkler system, which might have saved it.

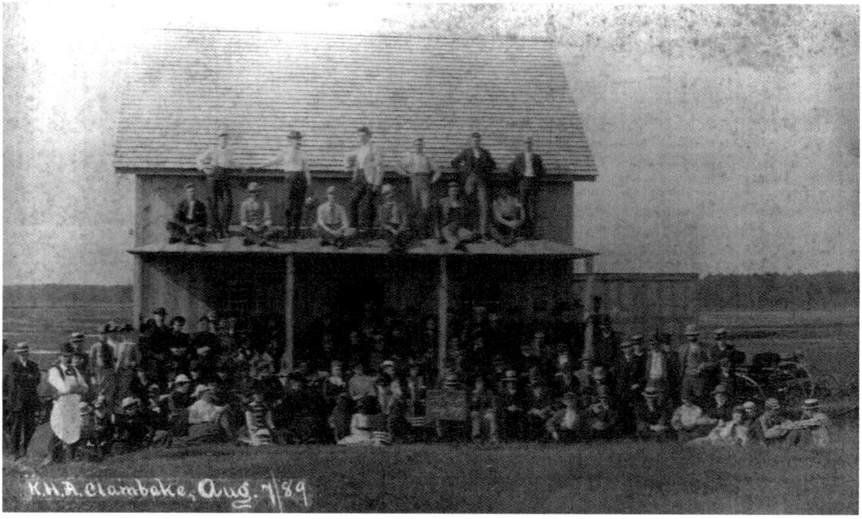

Club members posed for a photograph at the KHA clubhouse on Great Hill Road, in Kennebunk Beach, on August 7, 1889. The clubhouse no longer stands. The meaning of the club's initials was never revealed and remains a mystery. *Below*: Club members enjoy a clambake on the same day the photograph was taken.

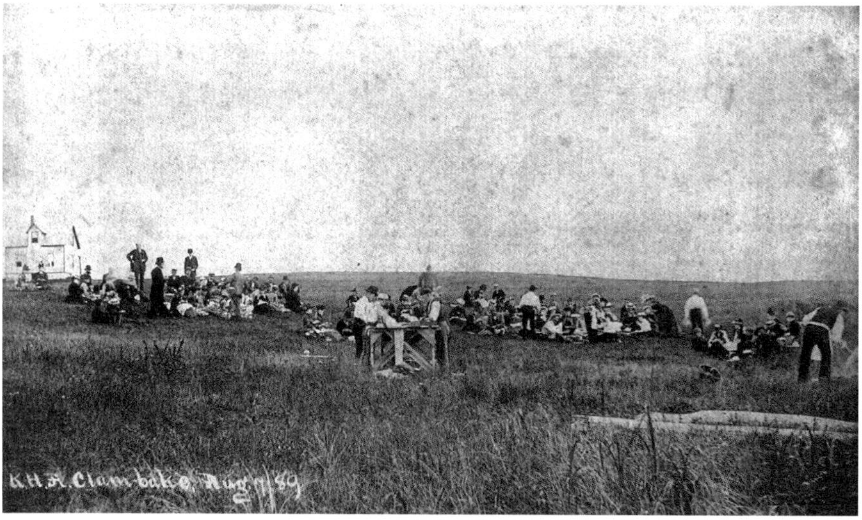

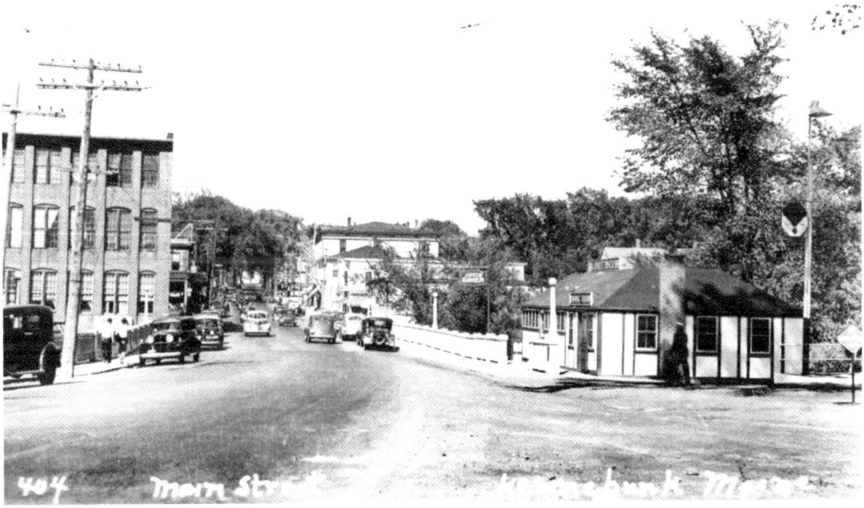

Jones Diner was a popular restaurant in Kennebunk and stood where Cumberland Farms is located today but was closer to the bridge that crosses the Mousam River. "Tinker" Jones, a former sheriff for York County, started the business and ran it with the help of his daughter, Doris Barker. Doris, with her husband, took it over when "Tink" retired. It was torn down in 1968.

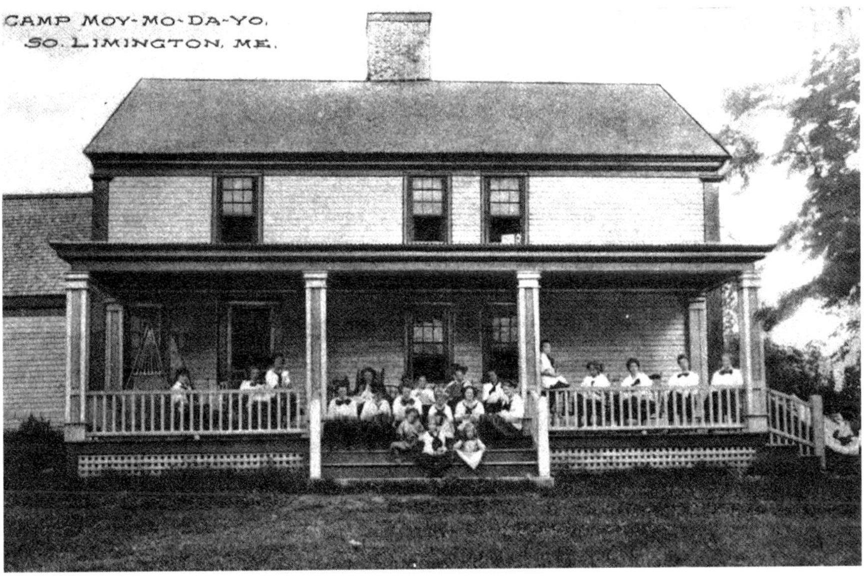

Camp Mo-Mo-Da-Yo was a girls' camp located in Limington that was started by two teachers, Elizabeth Moody and F. Helen Mayo. The name was a combination of the syllables of their names. Moody was a native of Limington, and the camp was started at this home in 1907. *Courtesy of Limington Historical Society.*

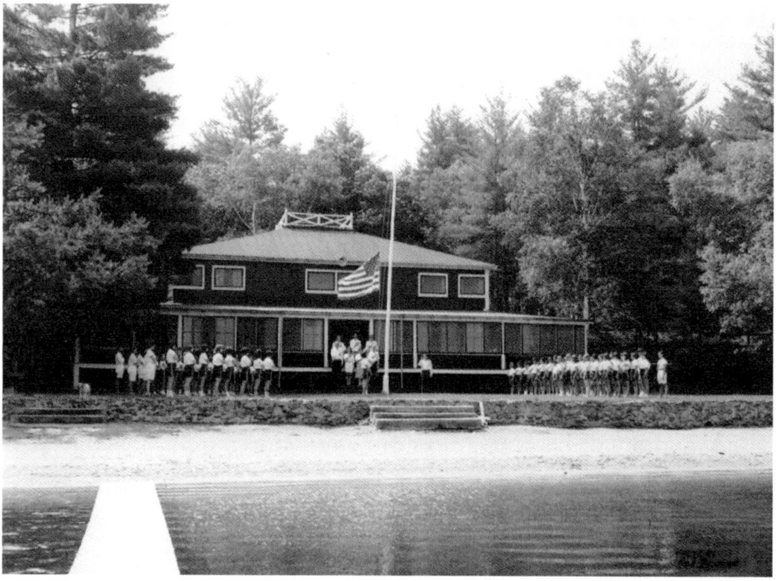

When the camp burned down on January 22, 1918, Moody and Mayo moved to Pequawket Pond, also known as Horne Pond. There, they built a new camp that continued to be popular with girls, many of whom returned summer after summer. *Courtesy of Limington Historical Society.*

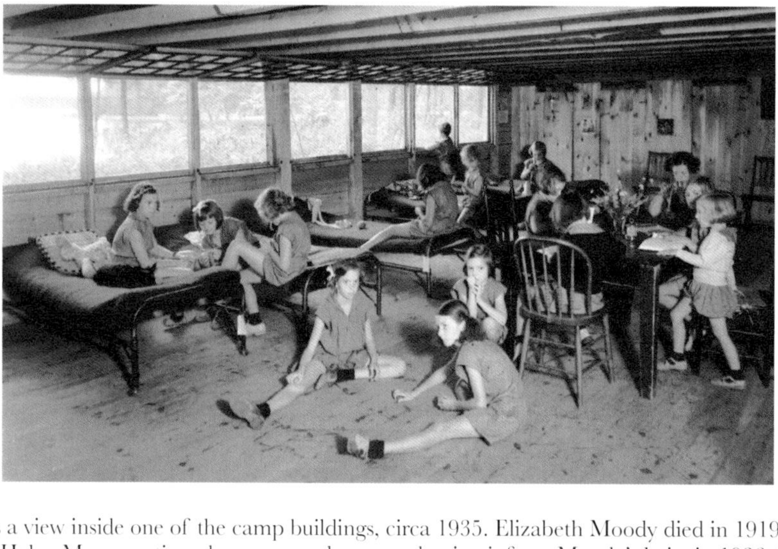

This a view inside one of the camp buildings, circa 1935. Elizabeth Moody died in 1919, and Helen Mayo continued to operate the camp, buying it from Moody's heirs in 1936. She formed a corporation to run the camp, also in 1936, and sold the camp to the corporation. The camp continued to operate after Helen's death, but by the late 1960s it was becoming financially difficult to keep it going. It was sold to the Downs Corporation in 1967, which ceased operations soon after. Today, nothing remains of the camp, and the land is now owned by the Town of Limington. *Courtesy of Limington Historical Society.*

CHAPTER FOUR

BUSINESSES AND INDUSTRY

This chapter contains images of local businesses, mills and factories that once dominated York County's towns and cities. The buildings that once housed these businesses are no longer standing or their purpose has changed over the years, and some have been altered beyond recognition. Commercial buildings are more likely to be altered or demolished as businesses close, move or expand. Many of the businesses in this chapter were family owned and operated, a trend that has vanished over the last thirty years as national retail stores have moved in. These lost buildings, factories and mills are examples of how state, national and global trends have changed the visual geography of York County over the last one hundred years.

The factories and mills that once operated in York County towns in the eighteenth through the early twentieth century were the primary source of income for the people who lived in those towns. Changing trends following the Second World War resulted in the closing of these factories, which left thousands unemployed. This also affected the towns in which the factories were located and resulted in business closings, empty storefronts and the loss of important architectural and historic structures. Starting in the 1950s, American companies began moving plant production from New England to the South, where labor was cheaper. Eventually these businesses were moved overseas, outsourcing products to places where they could be made cheaper than in the United States. The Goodall Mills in Sanford no longer exists, nor do the once thriving factories in Saco and Biddeford, many of which were located on Factory Island. Gone also are the smaller factories and mills that manufactured items needed for the larger mills, from bobbins to wooden crates. Water Street in Kennebunk is today a mixture of private homes, condominiums and businesses where thriving industries once stood.

In West Buxton, the lumber and box mills are long gone. Over fifty years later, Sanford, Biddeford and Saco still struggle to recover and find new identities.

Every Main Street in every York County town has suffered from these changes. While coastal towns have always had tourism to fall back on, inland towns have suffered the most. North Berwick's Main Street was once a bustling shopping center; today many of the remaining stores are empty and derelict or have been converted to apartments. In Berwick, there are no shops in Sullivan Square anymore and North Shapleigh Square doesn't exist today. Dock Square, in Kennebunkport, has had all its charm remodeled out of it. While Saco's Main Street thrives, Biddeford struggles to reinvent its Main Street, while at the same time promoting retail development on Route 111, far outside the downtown district.

Twenty-five years ago there wasn't a bank or large chain store in Waterboro; today all of those exist. Commercial development projects altered and replaced older homes and farms that had once stood along Route 1 from Kittery to the Scarborough town line. The heavily traveled roads and four-corner intersections of rural York County towns are now experiencing the same commercial growth that happened along Route 1. Rural York County is now vanishing at a catastrophic rate and will soon be gone.

For this chapter, I tried to locate a variety of businesses that have been lost in York County. Again, as I have stated before, plenty of images could be found for the coastal towns, but as I moved inland they became harder to locate. Regretfully, in trying to have a fair representation of all towns, some images had to be cut. For instance, an entire book could be done on lost buildings in Biddeford alone.

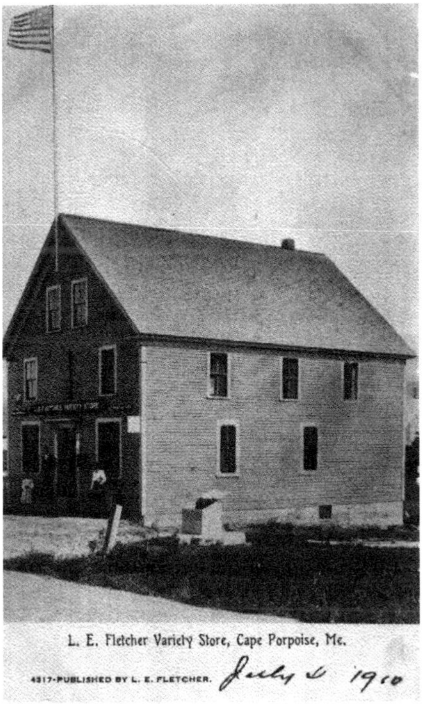

This image shows Luman Fletcher's store in Cape Porpoise about 1910. Built in 1893, Fletcher operated a grocery store here until his death in 1920. The trolley to Cape Porpoise passed right in front of the store, which was good for business. The store still stands, although much altered, as is expected with commercial buildings. Bradbury's Market is now located here.

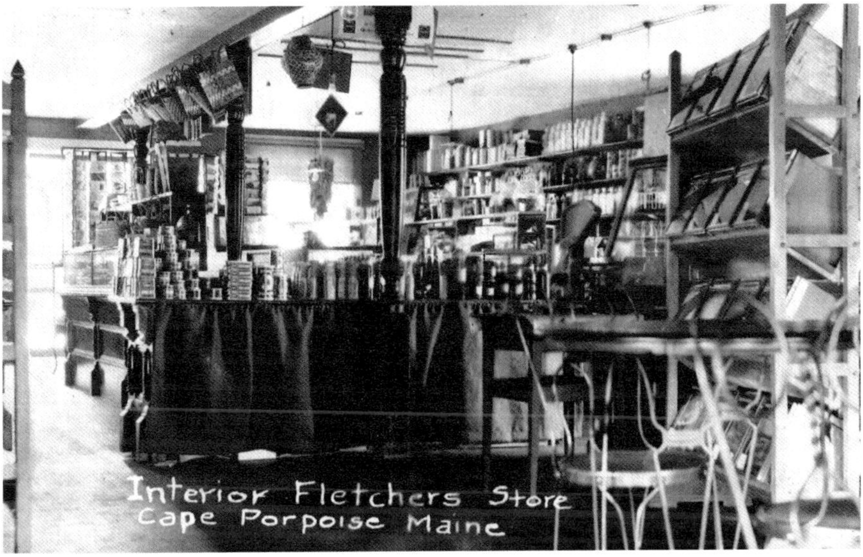

This is the interior of Fletcher's store as it appeared about 1910. In 1945, fire destroyed the interior of the store, which forced Bradbury's Market to close for several months. The Bradbury family, who bought the store in 1942, sold it in the 1970s, but it returned to the family when Thomas Bradbury and Steadman Seavy purchased the store in 1990.

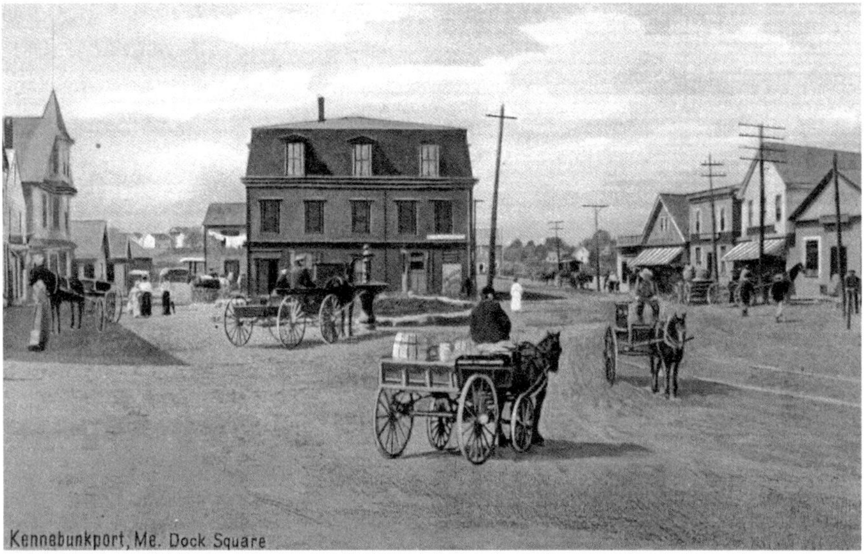

The tragedy of Kennebunkport's famed Dock Square is that while nearly every building in this postcard still stands, not one is recognizable today. This was a Victorian commercial district for a village changing rapidly from a seaport and shipbuilding town to a summer resort for the very wealthy. Not one building in this view predates 1870, yet within the last few years, every one of them has been virtually stripped to its frame and remodeled to look one hundred years older than it really is. The Dock Square of today is a Disney-like fantasy intended to attract large crowds of tourists to spend money in "Ye Olde Shops." The most obvious loss was the 1878 Brown Block, in the center of the photograph. An early bad remodeling of the building was removed several years ago, revealing the handsome Victorian detailing, which has now been replaced by lumberyard Colonial. Only two structures, neither visible here, retain their authentic appearance. The three-story Shingle-style Victorian building on the left was built as the town's post office in the 1880s. It has been sheared of all its Victorian features, shown here, and given a Colonial makeover. Over the years, Dock Square has had many looks and undergone many changes, and it would be unrealistic to expect it to still look like it did one hundred years ago. Still, what's missing in Dock Square today is honesty. Instead of acknowledging its true Victorian past, property owners have created a place that never actually existed.

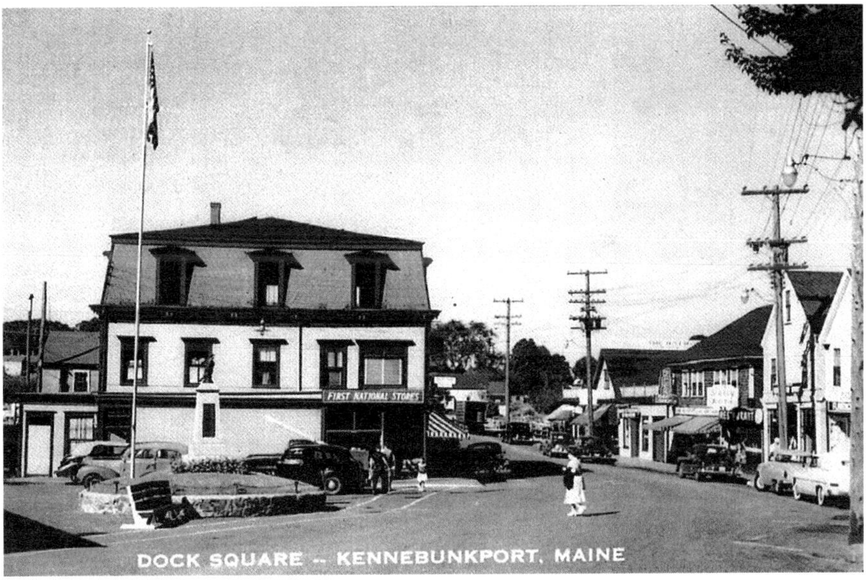

This image of Dock Square was taken circa 1955 and shows the Brown Block with its original siding and windows. You also see that the entrance was originally on the right side and not on the end facing you. This building has been remodeled several times, but this image gives you an idea of how the building once looked before it was "Colonialized."

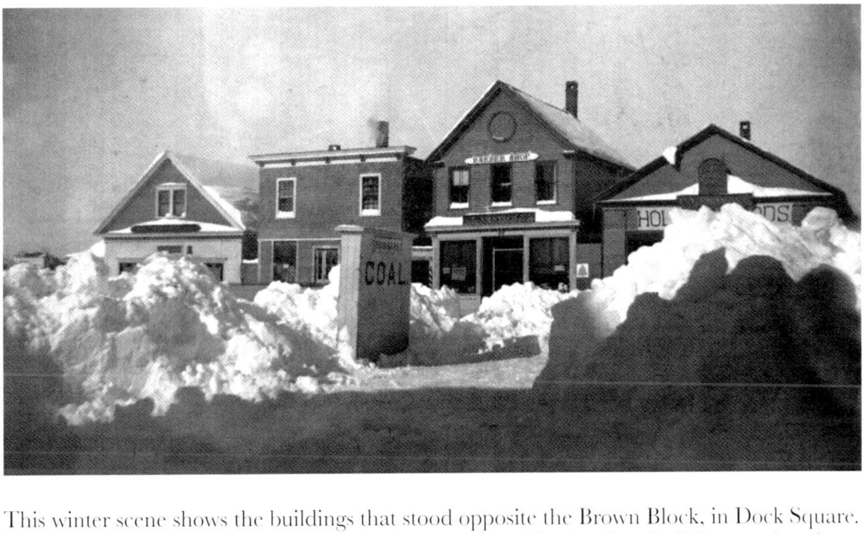

This winter scene shows the buildings that stood opposite the Brown Block, in Dock Square. After a fire in 1877 destroyed the businesses located on this site, these buildings replaced them. The stores on the far right and far left are gone, and the two in the center have been altered. Alison's Restaurant currently occupies the tall store building with the barbershop sign. I've shown several images here of Dock Square to give readers an idea of how it originally looked and how it has changed over the years. When you visit Dock Square today, you can see how fake it all seems.

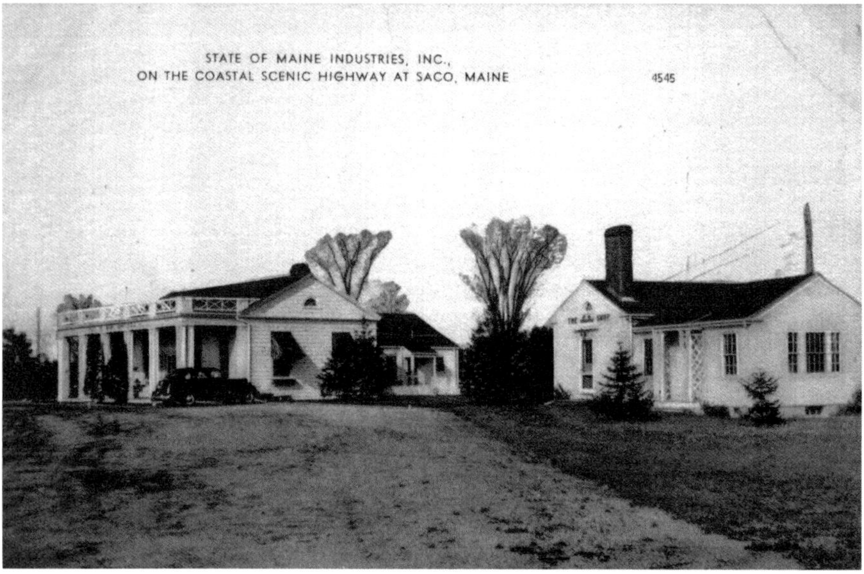

The Maine Industries building stood on Route 1 in Saco, approximately opposite Fun Town, and was razed for a car dealership after 2000. It was built circa 1940 and featured Maine-made items, from wooden lawn furniture to candy and other products. It was later used as the Biddeford-Saco Elks Lodge before it moved to its new location.

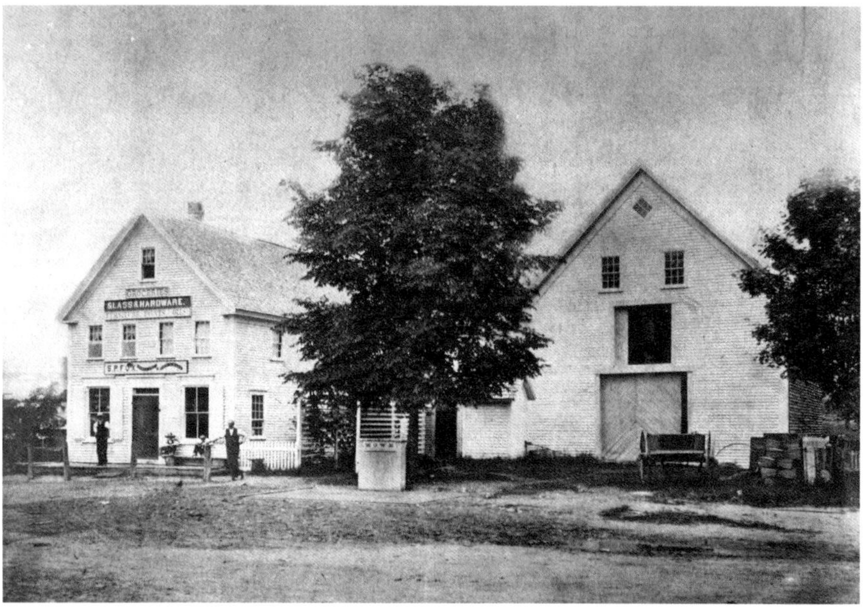

The S.P. Fox store, in Parsonsfield, shown here circa 1885, was owned by William Norton in 1898. He ran a grain store here. It was taken down around 1900 and replaced with the Norton Block. *Courtesy of Parsonsfield Porter Historical Society.*

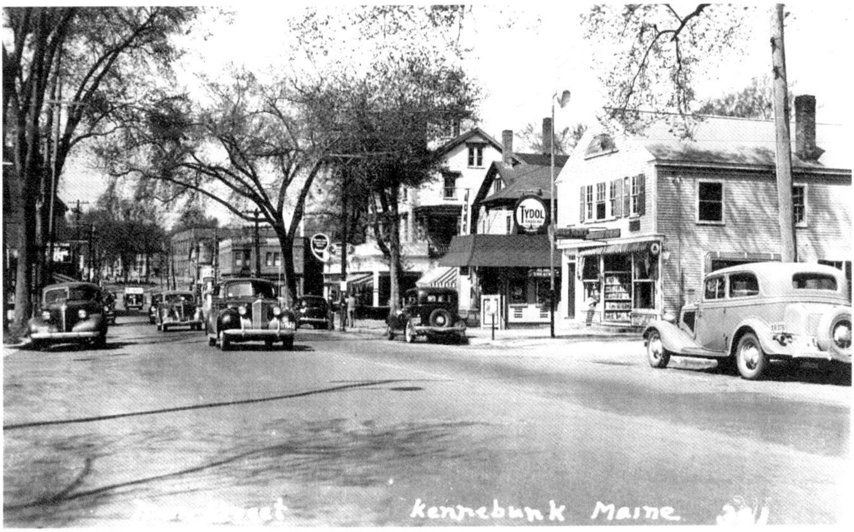

Main Street, in Kennebunk, circa 1940. None of these buildings still stand; they were demolished in 2000 and replaced with a really ugly building that is supposed to look Colonial but misses the mark by a long shot. I don't know why some architects think mixing different sidings and paint colors makes a building look like an eighteenth-century building, because it doesn't. The new building looks like something from the Southwest instead of New England. *Right to left*: the first building with the Tydol sign in front sold newspapers, bus tickets and had a lunch counter; the next building was the Anchor Theatre; followed by the Bowdoin Block with the Littlefield house on top. The house was raised in 1912 and the store block was built under it. It was a unique landmark that people noticed coming into downtown Kennebunk. Western Auto was later located there and operated by Author Jack for many years. His wife, Ruby Jack, ran a toy store on the very end. At one time, all these buildings were joined together to form Bowdoin's drugstore and gift shop.

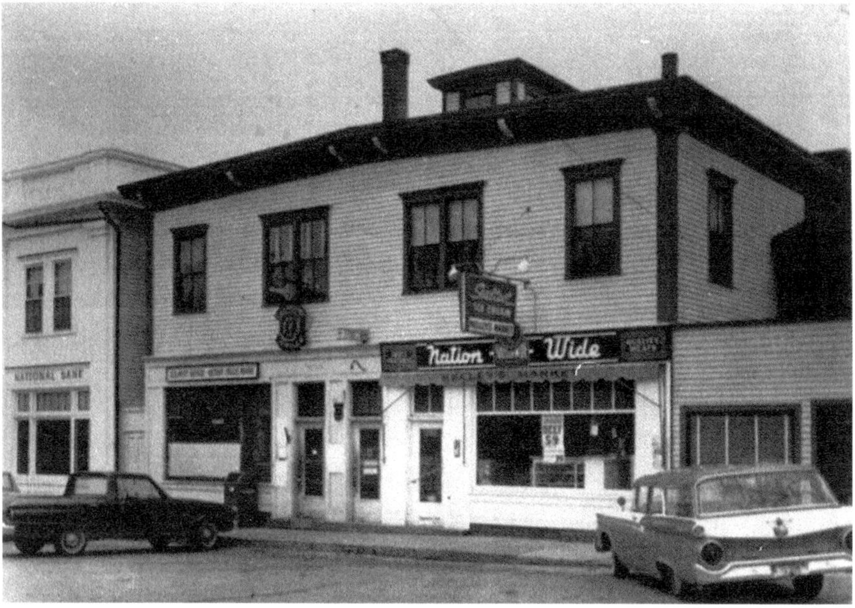

The Norton Block replaced the S.P. Fox store circa 1900. It stood on Federal Road, in Parsonsfield, next to the George W. Towle building, seen on the left. The Norton Block burned down in 1970. *Courtesy of Parsonsfield Porter Historical Society.*

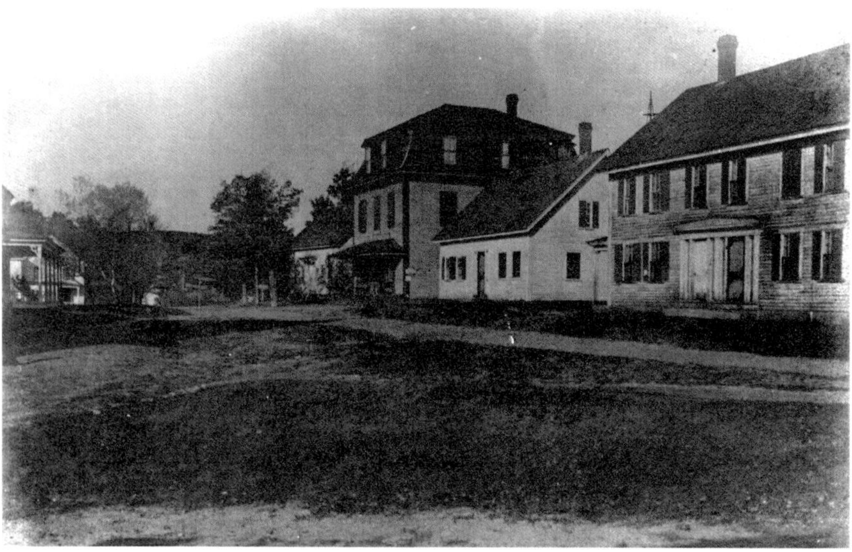

North Shapleigh Square, circa 1900. The building to the far left with the porch burned down in 1921. The three-story building, which housed a general store, and the home to its right both burned down in 1972.

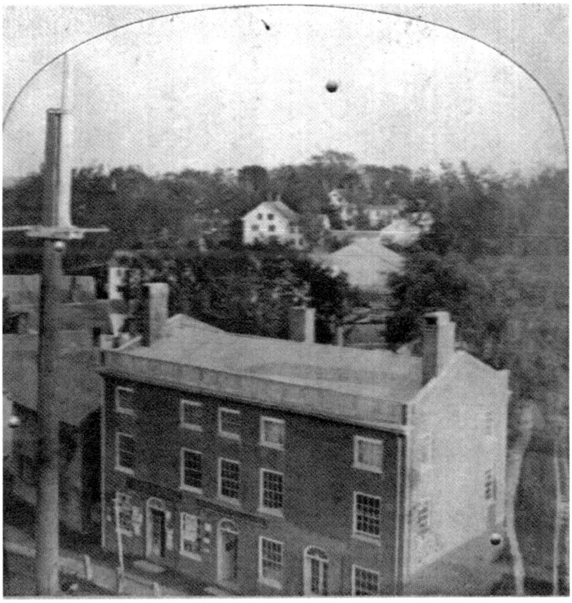

The Warren-Kelly block originally stood where Kennebunk's town hall now stands. It was a three-story brick Federal-style building built around 1815. In 1920, it was moved across the street, a slow process that took several days. It later became the IGA Store. The top floor burned and was removed, and the remaining building was demolished in 1987 for a parking lot.

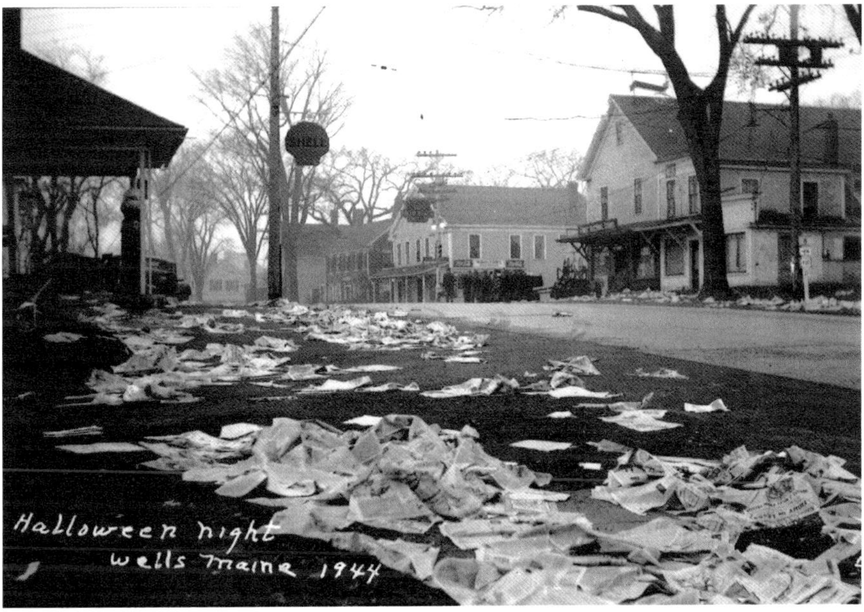

This image shows Wells Corner on November 1, 1944, following a Halloween prank that left the area littered with newspaper. Route 109 is between the buildings on the right where the men are standing. The two buildings on the right were demolished for a gas station, and the store behind the men has been mutilated and now houses a pizza shop. Ocean National Bank now stands where Shell Station stood, on the left.

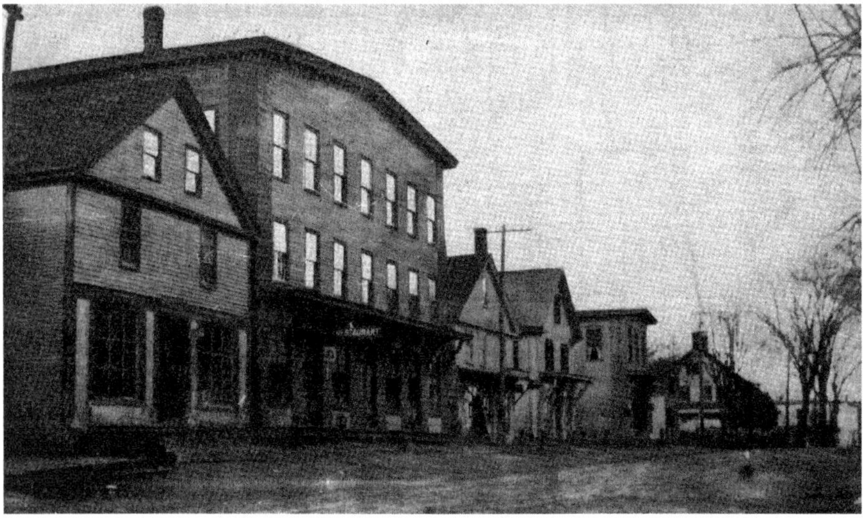

This is the south side of Main Street in North Berwick. The first three buildings no longer stand, and the house at the end is gone; Cumberland Farms is located there today.

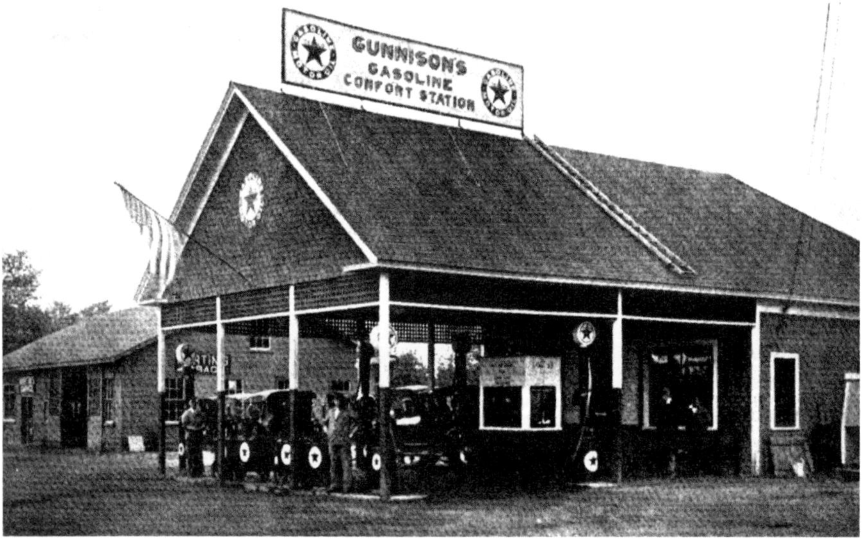

Gunnison's Gasoline Comfort Station in Kittery, Maine, circa 1920, was typical of service stations constructed during the period. This is a great image in which you can see the pumps with cars lined up for gas. The attendants are all posed for the photograph and everything looks neat and clean.

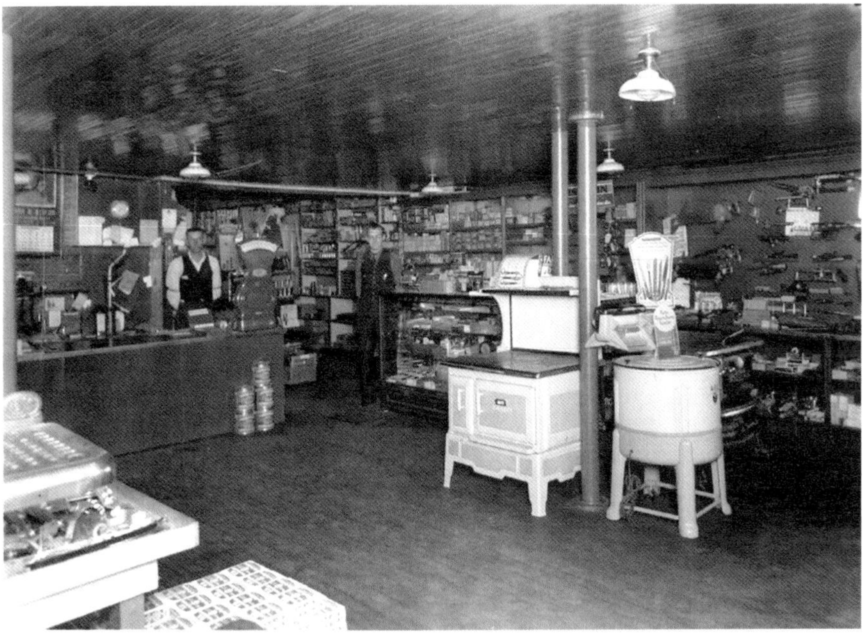

This wonderful photograph was taken inside the Norton hardware store once located in Kezar Falls. The two men in the picture are Clarence Sawyer and Neil Hamilton, who bought the business in 1930. *Courtesy of Parsonsfield Porter Historical Society.*

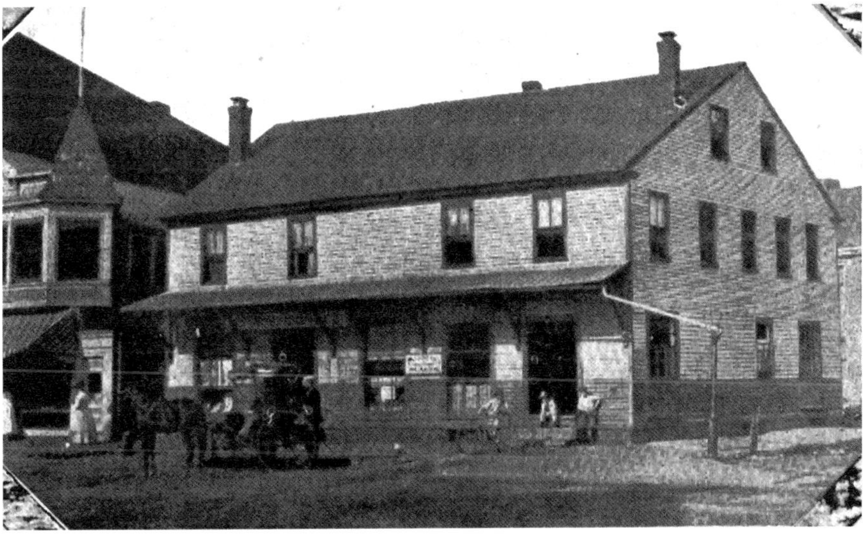

This store was built circa 1830 by Job Harris and brothers Samuel and Thomas Parks and was located on Sullivan Square, Berwick, to the right of Spence & Mathews Insurance building. In 1871, the post was opened here and remained at this location for many years. The town's hay scales were on the left of the store. Johnson's Market, operated by Forrest and Helen Johnson, moved here in 1963.

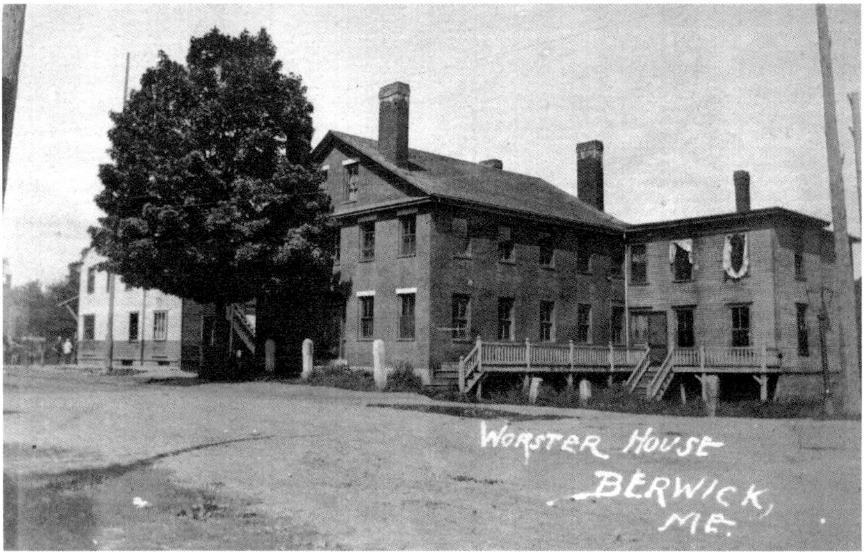

This building was originally known as the Worcester House and was located next to Back Street, in Berwick. Jason Tibbettes started a hardware store here in 1913, and John Bell bought the business in 1930 and changed the name to Bell's Hardware. Maurice Martel bought it in 1963 and ran the business for many years. The building was later torn down. *Courtesy of Brian Cincotta.*

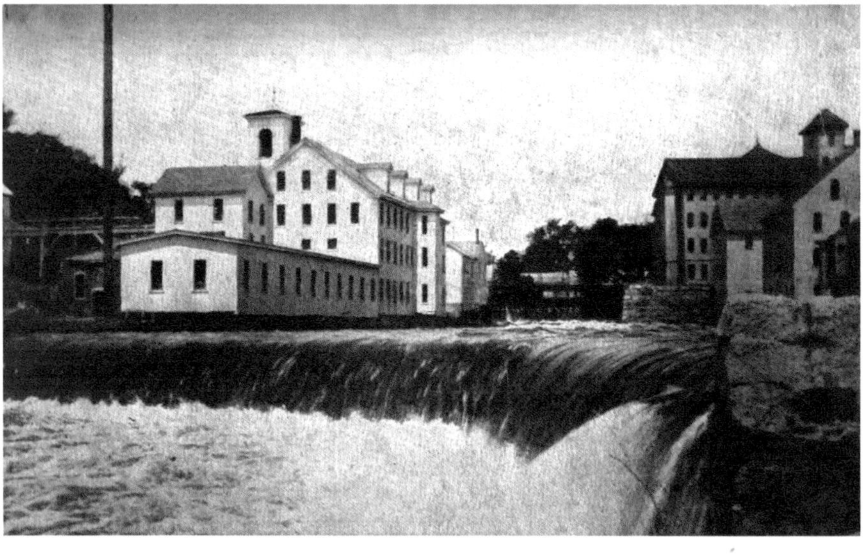

This building, in Kennebunk, stood behind today's Cumberland Farms and was built in 1868. It was leased to the Union Lace Company, maker of shoe string and lace. In 1883, a roller-skating rink opened on the third floor. It became a paper mill in 1896 when the Leatheroid Manufacturing Company began making paper. It was demolished in 1922. *Courtesy of Greg Hubbard.*

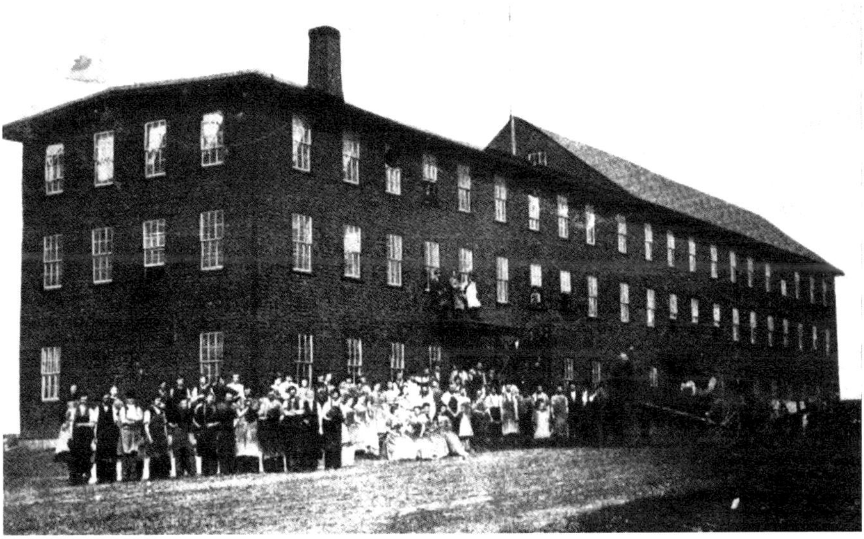

Nute Shoe Shop was located in Berwick, on the river. L.M. and D.H. Nute built this building in 1871. The shop closed about 1889 and was converted to tenements in 1896. It no longer stands. *Courtesy of Brian Cincotta.*

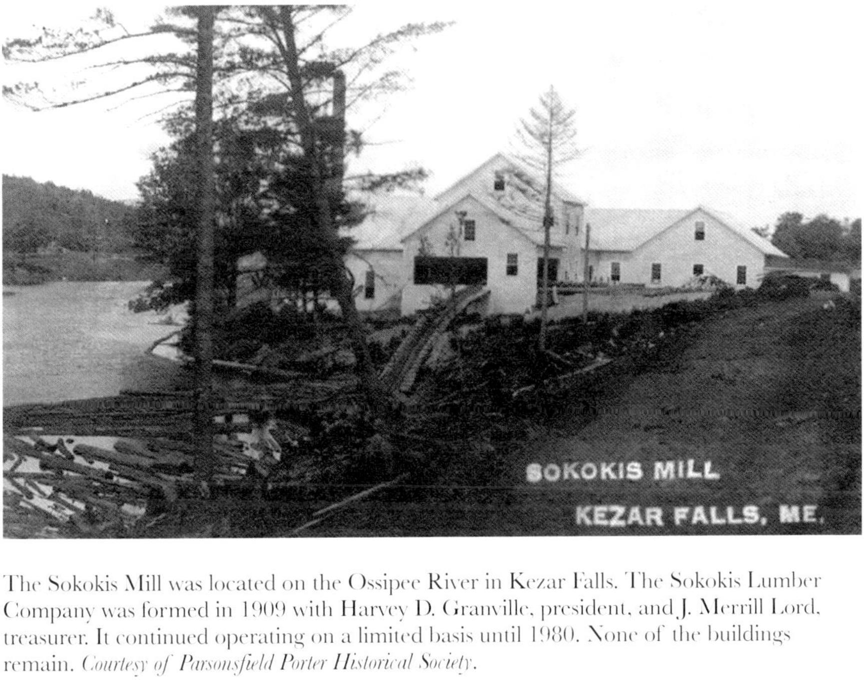

The Sokokis Mill was located on the Ossipee River in Kezar Falls. The Sokokis Lumber Company was formed in 1909 with Harvey D. Granville, president, and J. Merrill Lord, treasurer. It continued operating on a limited basis until 1980. None of the buildings remain. *Courtesy of Parsonsfield Porter Historical Society.*

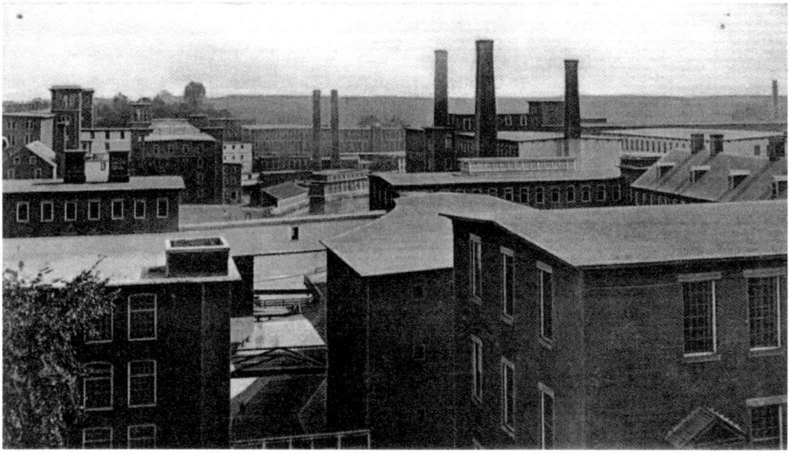

The Laconia Mills in Biddeford merged with the Pepperell Mill in 1899. This was the largest merger in the county at the time. Laconia became the blanket division, while Pepperell manufactured sheets. The York Mills became part of Bates Manufacturing and were closed in 1958. The Lincoln Street Mill closed in 1969. Several of the buildings seen here in these two images have been demolished, while the remaining buildings have been turned into condominiums or retail businesses. *Courtesy of McArthur Library.*

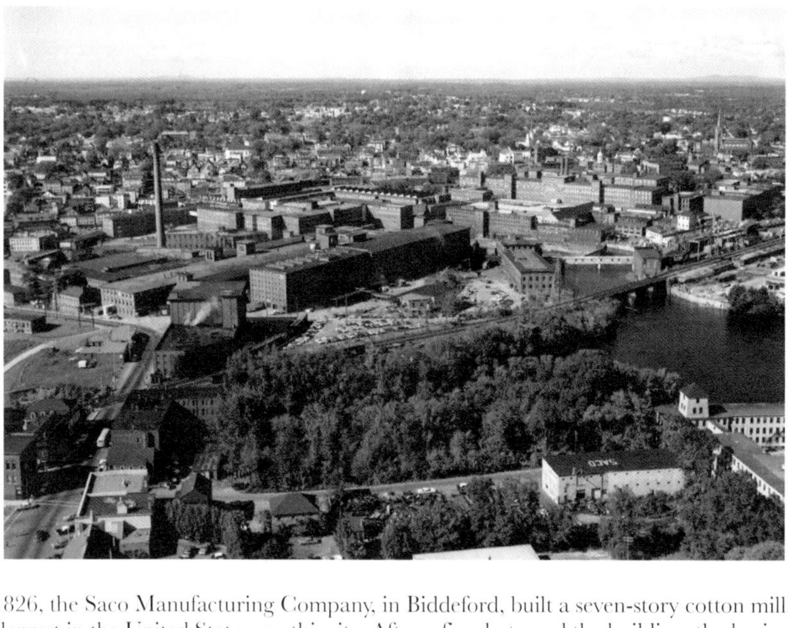

In 1826, the Saco Manufacturing Company, in Biddeford, built a seven-story cotton mill, the largest in the United States, on this site. After a fire destroyed the building, the business was reorganized as the York Manufacturing Company. The establishment of the Laconia Mills in 1844 and Pepperell Mill in 1850 made the combined mill district one of the largest cotton milling complexes in the country.

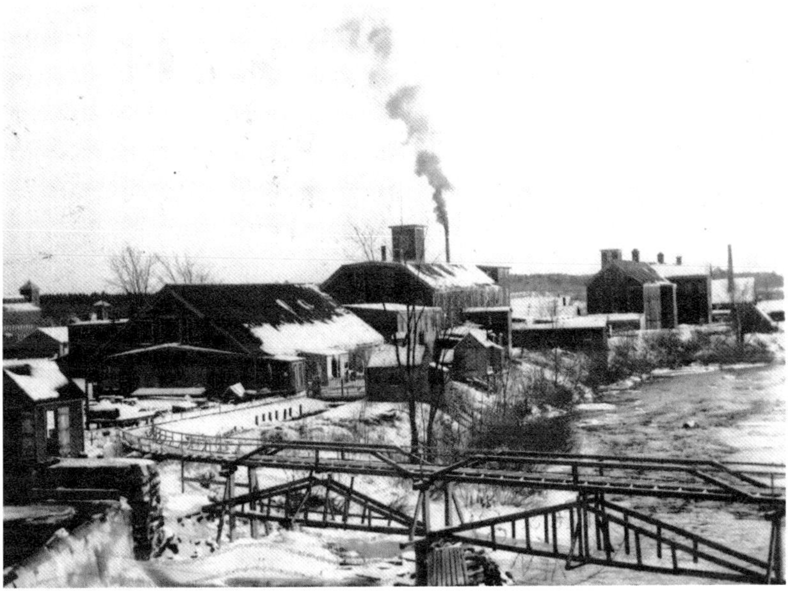

This image, circa 1895, is looking down Water Street in Kennebunk toward the factories that once stood between the street and the Mousam River. The footbridge connected the factories on Water Street to the paper mill on the other side of the river. The buildings on the left belonged to the Leatheroid Manufacturing Company and the buildings farther down on the right to the Mousam Manufacturing Company.

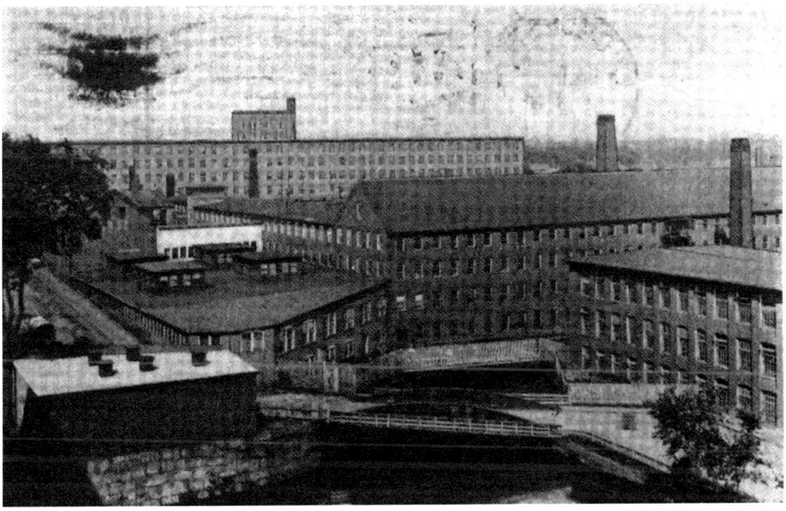

The Saco-Pettee machine shop, shown here circa 1905, was located in Biddeford, across from Factory Island. Saco-Pettee began operation in the 1880s and was a producer of high-quality textile machinery. Saco-Pettee merged with the Lowell Machine Shop in 1912, creating the Saco-Lowell shops. The Saco-Lowell machine shop became the largest textile machinery company in the country.

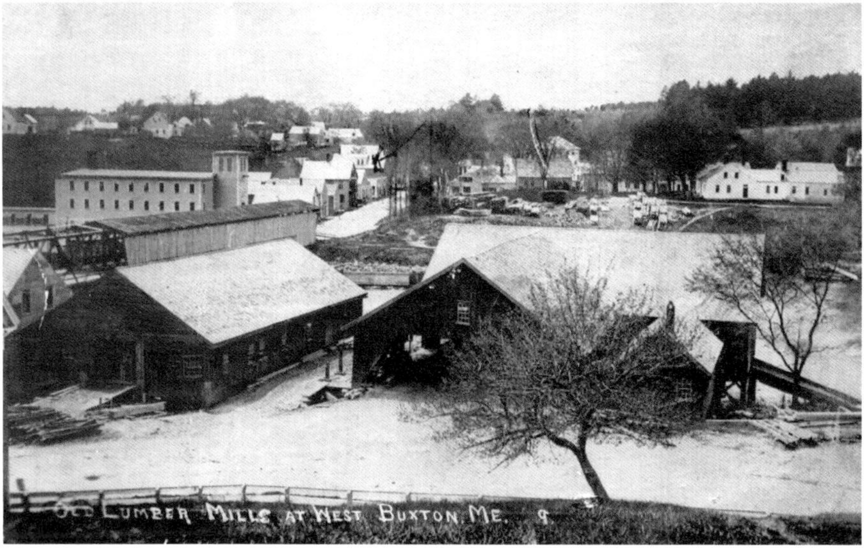

West Buxton sawmills, circa 1900, stood beside the Saco River across from Bar Mills. The buildings in this photograph are (left to right): Hanover's woolen mill, the old covered bridge, just visible is the gristmill, the heading mill, main sawmill, log chute and Gilman's file house. *Courtesy of Buxton-Hollis Historical Society.*

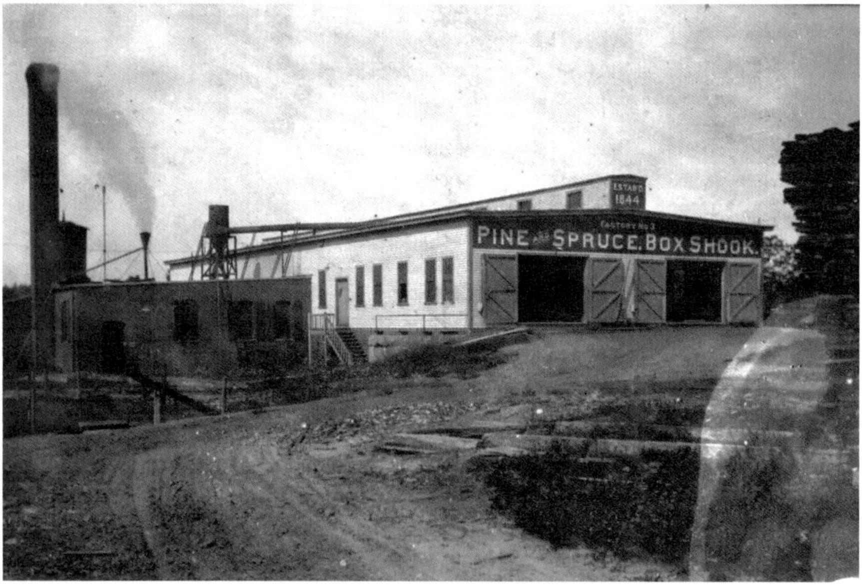

The Pine and Spruce Box Shook Company was established in 1844 and was located near the bridge that connects West Buxton with Bar Mills. It made wooden boxes to be used to send products out to retailers. *Courtesy of Buxton-Hollis Historical Society.*

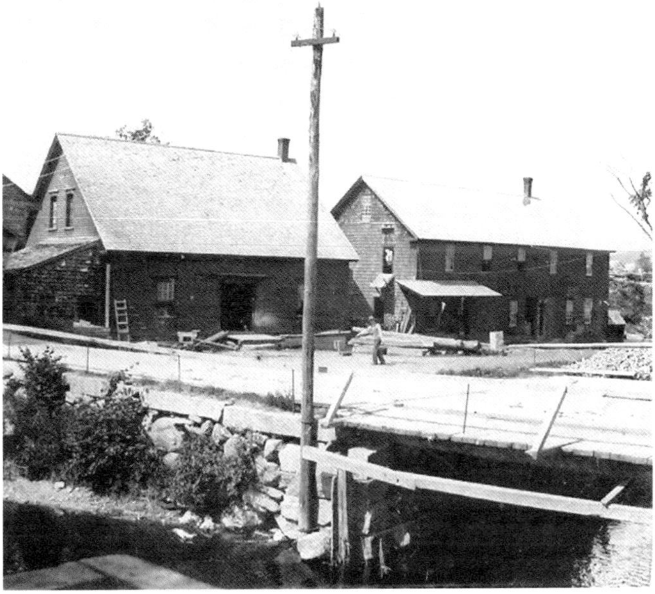

The Devereux gristmill, on the left, and the Bobbin factory, on the right, stood at the end of the Kezar Falls Bridge, on the Parsonsfield side of the Ossipee River. The gristmill was built in 1871 and the bobbing factory was built in 1878 by J. Merrifield. The mill manufactured bobbins for woolen mills for many years. *Courtesy of Parsonsfield Porter Historical Society*.

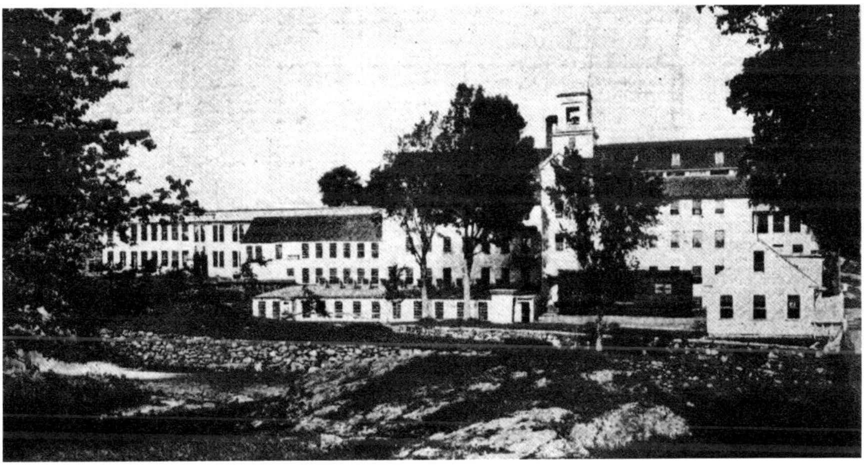

The Alpaca Mill, in Springvale. The original section on the right, with the tower, was built in 1842 and was used to manufacture wool. The sections to the left were added after 1873. The Maine Alpaca Company, a division of the Goodall enterprise, bought the mill in 1899. The original mill was demolished in 1926 and the remaining sections were torn down in the 1980s. A housing development known as Haven Green now occupies the site.

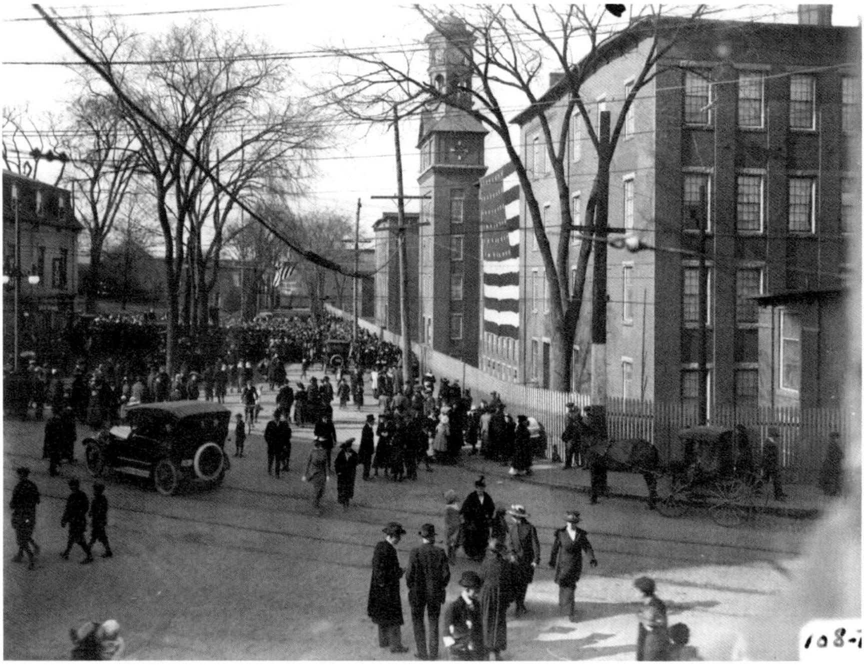

Flag Day, April, 14, 1917, showing the clock tower of the Lincoln Mill, in Biddeford. The large flag on the mill was borrowed from the Filene's Company in Boston; it measured fifty by one hundred feet and weighed three hundred pounds. The clock tower, one of Biddeford's most significant landmarks, was removed by owners Gordon McDonald and Michael Scott, who felt that saving the clock was a luxury they couldn't afford. Losing the clock tower is equal to the loss of Union Station in Portland. McDonald and Scott have been rehabilitating the Lincoln Mill for several years, but removing the clock tower was an unthinkable act of vandalism. It was another architectural and historical loss in a string of losses that the city of Biddeford has suffered in recent years. A group was formed to raise the $40,000 needed to repair and save the clock in place. That the money could not be raised shows how little the people of Biddeford care about their history, as $40,000 was not a lot of money and should have been easily raised. When it wasn't, the clock was removed, and its current location is unknown. *Courtesy of McArthur Library.*

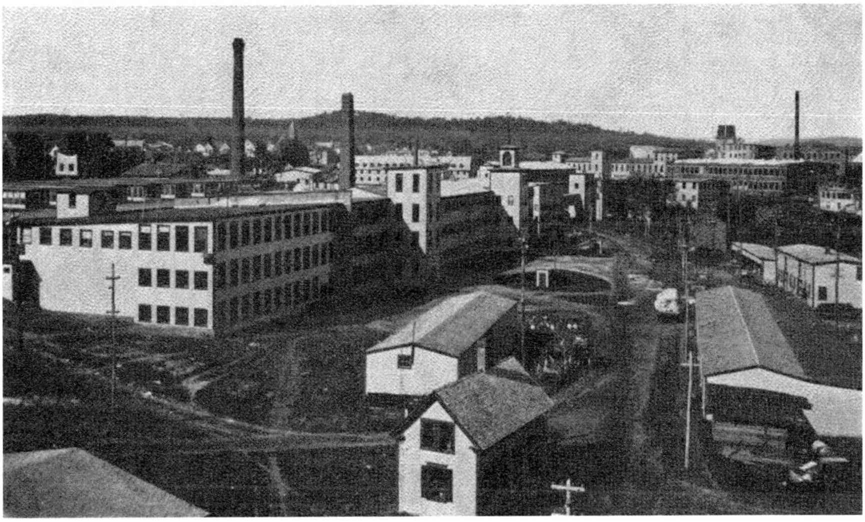

After selling his mill in Troy, New Hampshire, which had made horse blankets, Thomas Goodall came to Sanford and established the Goodall Mills in 1867. His factory was built alongside Mousam River and first made carriage robes and blankets. It would later expand to manufacture mohair plush, which was in demand for upholstering railroad seats and making carpets. Eventually the mills manufactured fabric for military uniforms and Palm Beach fabric for summer suits. Goodall's textiles were known for their brilliant and fast colors and found buyers worldwide. The success of the mill, which was run by Thomas Goodall's three sons after his death, resulted in rapid growth and expansion. This image dates to circa 1910, before the Goodalls began replacing their early wooden mill buildings with buildings made of brick and concrete block. Between 1915 and 1925, the entire business was rebuilt, a feat that required removing a hill and fifty-five thousand yards of soil, sand and rock. The Goodall Worsted, as the mills had become known, merged with the Sanford Mills in 1944. In 1954, Burlington Mills, then the largest textile firm in the country, bought Sanford Mills. It moved the Sanford production to its mills in the South and then closed the mills. This left close to four thousand people unemployed and two million square feet of empty mills vacant. Some of the factory buildings have been demolished, while others are still abandoned and awaiting rehabilitation.

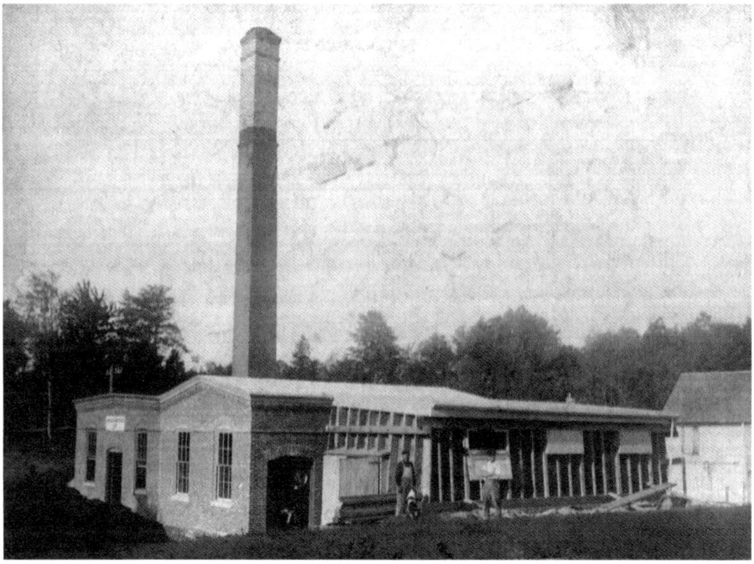

The Mousam Water Company was created in 1895 to supply water from Branch Brook to Kennebunk homes. In 1921, the water company was absorbed into the new Kennebunk, Kennebunkport, Wells Water District. Eventually a new pumping station was built to replace this early one.

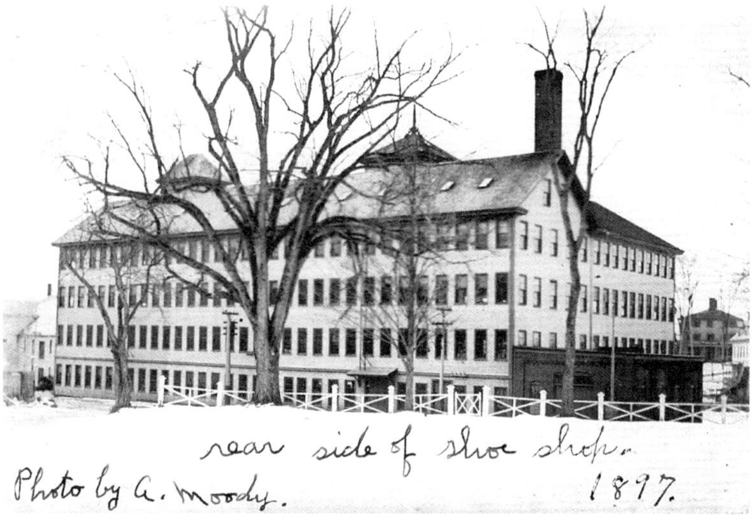

The Davis Shoe Shop, with additions, dominated the corner of Storer and Main Streets in Kennebunk until 1903. Built in 1877, Joseph Davis moved his shoe factory into the building from Mechanic Falls, Maine. Later, two large additions were constructed, one in 1884 and another in 1885. The building was vacant in 1903 when a fire destroyed the mill and all the buildings on the other three corners.

CHAPTER FIVE

SCHOOLS AND CHURCHES

As you read this chapter, you may be struck by the number of schools and churches that have been lost to fire. Several burned due to arson, including a few destroyed by children. Most likely poorly cleaned chimneys were the cause of some of the fires.

Once fires started, they were difficult to control and extinguish. Rural York County lacked the more sophisticated firefighting equipment owned by many of Maine's cities. As a result, fire departments relied on lakes, rivers and small streams to provide water to put out fires. But this was impossible during the winter, as such sources froze. A few communities had fire hydrants, but valves were not standardized and thus did not necessarily fit the hose couplings from all nearby fire departments. The Old Orchard Beach fire of 1907 was devastating in part due to this problem. Rural towns could not easily afford modern equipment, and most simply hoped for the best.

The fire of 1947 changed all of that. When that fire swept through York County, towns found themselves helpless and unable to contain the fires. The one good thing that came out of that fire was that afterward, towns were better prepared and had the necessary equipment to ensure that a similar fire wouldn't happen again. There were many fundraisers after the fire to raise money for the small towns of York County to allow them to purchase new, modern equipment. Of course, the causes of the fire of 1947 are more complex than outdated equipment. Joyce Butler's book *Wildfire Loose: The Week Maine Burned* examines the fire in more detail.

It is more difficult to pinpoint the origins of church fires, although one frequent cause was steeples being hit by lightning. Later, when stoves were installed, poorly maintained chimneys probably resulted in many fires, just like those in the schools. The Saco Congregational Church burned down in 2000 because the workers stripping the church didn't follow basic safety measures while using flammable paint strippers. The First Baptist Church in North Berwick burned down, along with several other buildings on Main Street, in 1906. Churches also burned down in Wells, Cape Porpoise, Fortune's Rock, Biddeford, Wells Branch and Newfield, to name a few towns.

The buildings in this chapter that didn't burn down were demolished after they no longer served the function that they were originally built for or were deemed unfit for commercial development. Many of the churches fell into disrepair due to lack of funds and dwindling congregations, and this resulted in many buildings simply falling apart and being demolished, like the Methodist church in Kennebunkport.

Biddeford's St. Mary's School, an important landmark, was demolished for a Dunkin' Donuts, and Birch Street School was lost due to ignorance and laziness. Newer, modern schools replaced many of the early one-room schoolhouses, which were then abandoned. Many of the older schools were replaced or demolished in the 1960s and 1970s following a tragic fire in Chicago on December 1, 1958, which destroyed the Catholic elementary school Our Lady of the Angels. Ninety-three children and three nuns perished in the fire. Their deaths resulted because the interior was made almost entirely of combustible material. The wooden floors had been coated and recoated many times with flammable petroleum-based waxes. There were only two fire alarms in the school and only four fire extinguishers that were mounted seven feet off the floor, out of reach of the adults and all of the children. The only fire escape was locked and inaccessible. After the fire, communities around the country enacted new building codes and laws to prevent this tragedy from happening again. York County towns saw an increase in new school construction and remodeling in the two decades following the Chicago fire.

Finally, this chapter includes photographs from the Shaker Village that once existed in Alfred. Unlike the Sabbath Day Shaker Village in Poland, Maine, which has been preserved and is open to the public, the Alfred Shakers have largely been forgotten. Of the sixty-five original buildings, only eight survive, although much altered. Today, the Friends of the Alfred Shakers Museum work to preserve the memory of the Alfred Shakers and have restored a carriage shed that now functions as a museum.

The Shakers' history dates back to the mid-1700s, when a small religious group in Manchester, England, adopted the practice of shaking, dancing and whirling during religious meetings. They believed that these rituals were an indication of being possessed by spirits, a state they believed was a sacred experience. This group was led by a young woman named Ann Lee, who was known as "Mother Ann." Inspired by a vision, she led a band of her followers to the New World to seek religious freedom. They first settled in Albany, New York, in 1776, but their growing popularity meant that they needed to expand, so they founded new groups in New England. The Shaker community in Alfred was organized in 1793. At its peak, the community in Alfred had over two hundred members; however, by 1900, it had dwindled to thirty-nine. The remaining buildings are now owned by the Brothers of Christian Instruction, who purchased the village when the remaining Shakers sold it in 1931. The Shakers were not given tax exemption like other churches were, and as a result, when buildings were no longer needed they were torn down or sold and moved away.

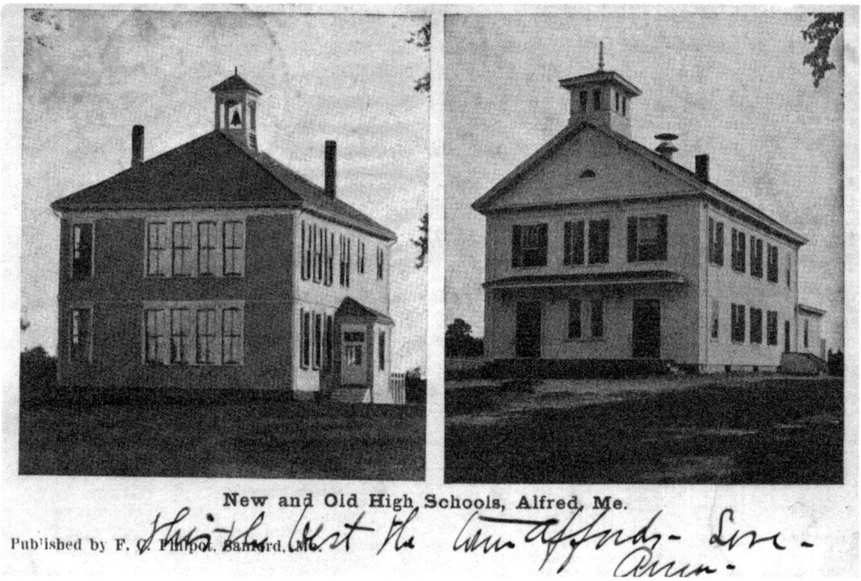

The Alfred School, on the right, housed the high school and grammar classes and was built in 1862. It burned down on September 27, 1904, and was replaced by the school building on the left, which no longer stands.

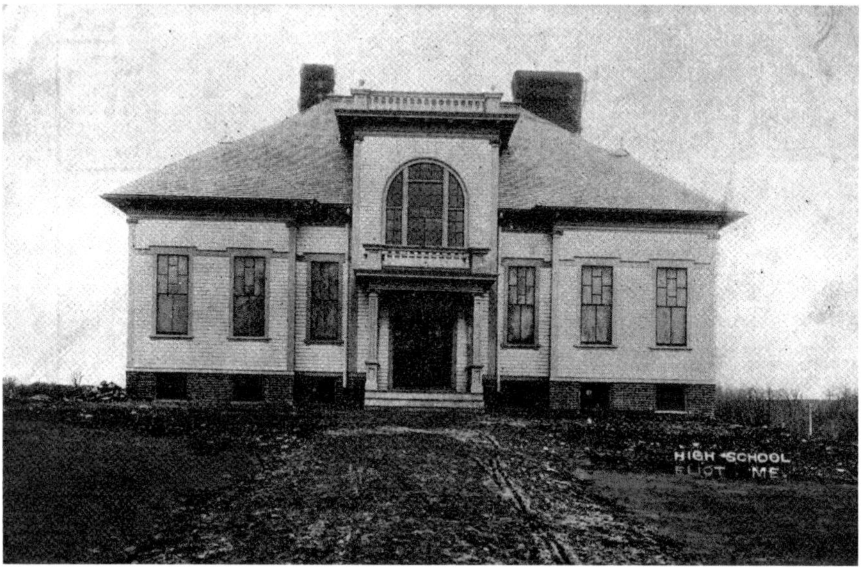

First called the Central School, and later Eliot High School, this institution was built in 1906. It was designed by Alvah T. Ramsdell, who lived in York. It was used as a school until 1946, at which time it became the town hall until 1987, when it was demolished.

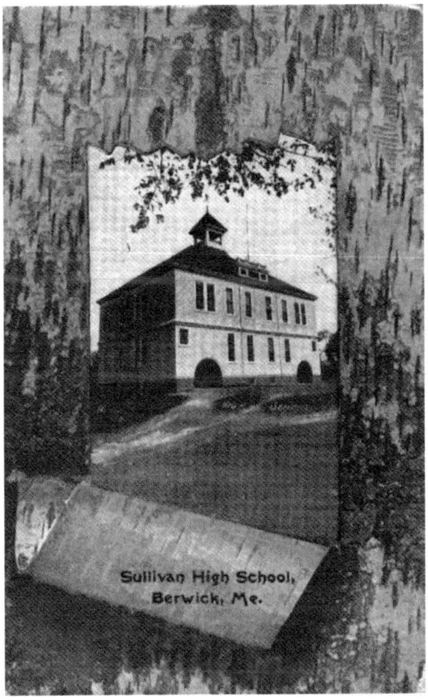

Sullivan School, in Berwick, was built in 1894–95 and replaced a school that had stood on the same site until it burned. Sullivan Street, Sullivan Square and the high school were named after the Sullivan family, who were early settlers to Berwick. Sullivan High School burned down on June 6, 1927, and was replaced by a brick school that still stands but has been closed for several years.

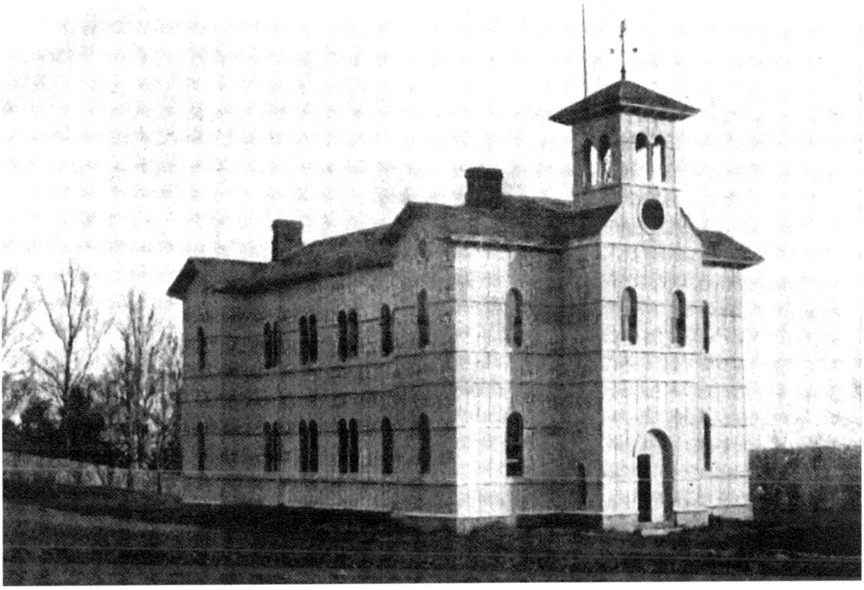

Berwick Academy, a private school, is located in South Berwick and was founded in 1791. Throughout its history, various buildings have come and gone as the academy has grown. This stark, angular Italian Revival building was designed by Richard Upjohn. This is where noted nineteenth-century writer Sarah Orne Jewett went to school. This building was moved back when the Fog Memorial building was built in 1893–94 and was later torn down.

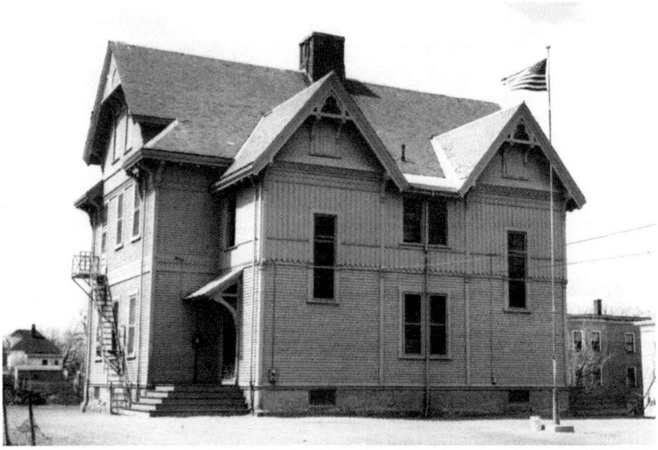

Built in 1891 and designed in the Stick style, Birch Street School, in Biddeford, had four classrooms on two floors. St. James School, a private Catholic school, acquired the building from the city for additional classroom space. It let the school fall into such disrepair that it had to be closed. City council members were so determined to destroy the building, which was eligible for National Landmark status, that they produced structural engineering reports stating that the building was unsafe. However, independent studies by preservationists proved the city's reports to be false. Efforts to save the building were to no avail; the school was burned for fire practice and the site was made into a parking lot for St. James School. *Courtesy of McArthur Library.*

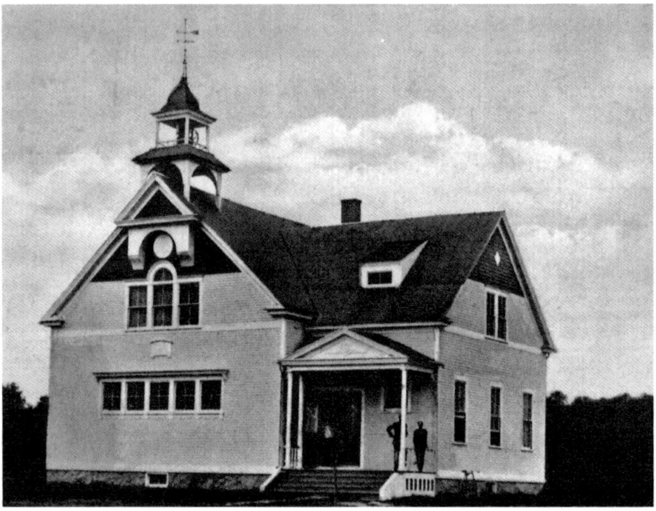

Wells High School, built in 1901, was supposedly designed by local architect William Barry. It was the first consolidated school in Wells and Ogunquit. Previously, high school classes had been held in different schools around town. It stood where the current junior high school is now located on Route 1.

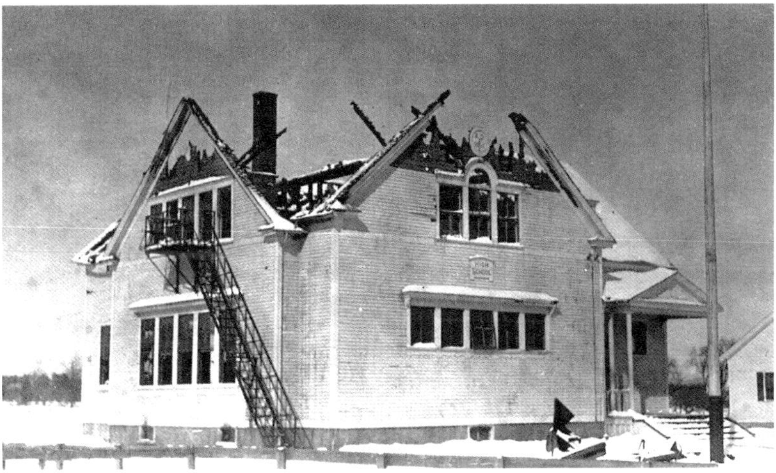

Wells High School, shown here, was partially burned in 1909 and then rebuilt to two full stories. It burned again in 1922 and was rebuilt and used until a larger brick school was built in 1937.

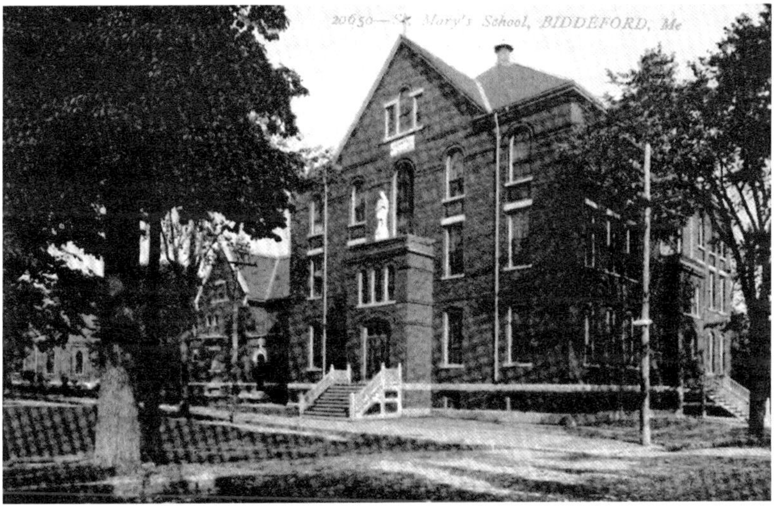

Another Biddeford landmark that has been lost is St. Mary's School, built in 1892, and St. Mary's Convent, built in 1906. They were destroyed in 2001 by developer Steven Sparangis for a Dunkin' Donuts. Biddeford seems to be determined to demolish its history building by building, ignoring the lessons that other cities have learned after losing their landmarks. Still, the people of Biddeford put on a good show, standing by as the building was destroyed, wringing their hands, shrugging their shoulders and saying how tragic it all was. St. Mary's was an important historical and religious landmark that was once the center of Catholic life in the city. Francis Fassett, who designed some of the state's most important buildings in the late nineteenth century, designed St. Mary's.

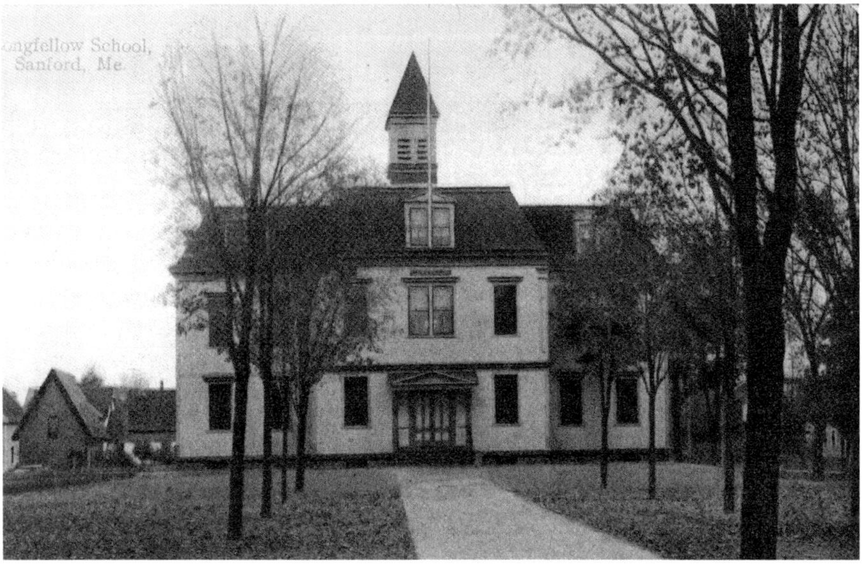

Longfellow School, in Sanford, was an elegant wooden school typical of those built in the Victorian era. It housed both the high school and lower grades and was named for the poet Henry Wadsworth Longfellow. Ernest Goodall, of the Sanford Goodalls, provided the funds for its construction in 1888. It stood on School Street, near the post office, and was demolished in 1971.

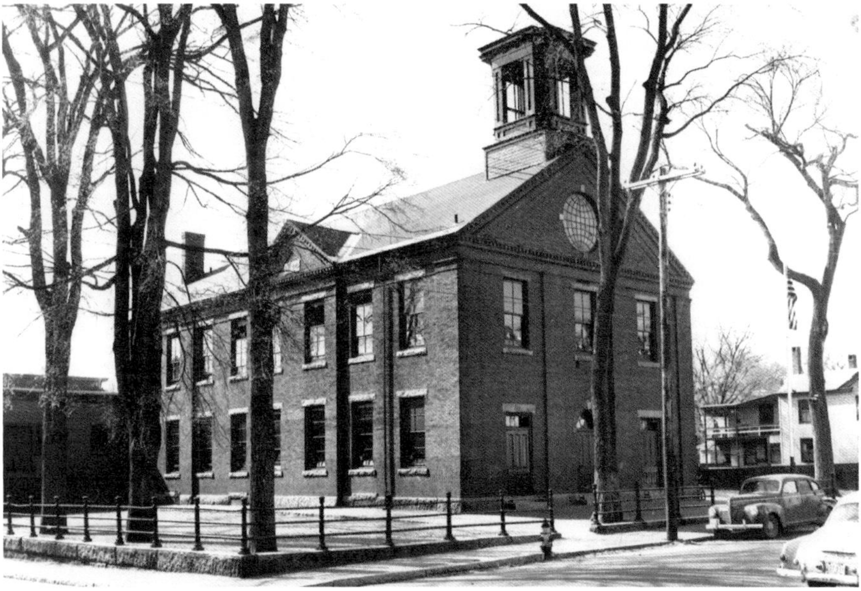

The Washington Street School, in Biddeford, was built in 1848 and first housed the high school. In 1888, after a new high school was built on Alfred Street, it became a grammar school. It was torn down in June 1967. *Courtesy of McArthur Library.*

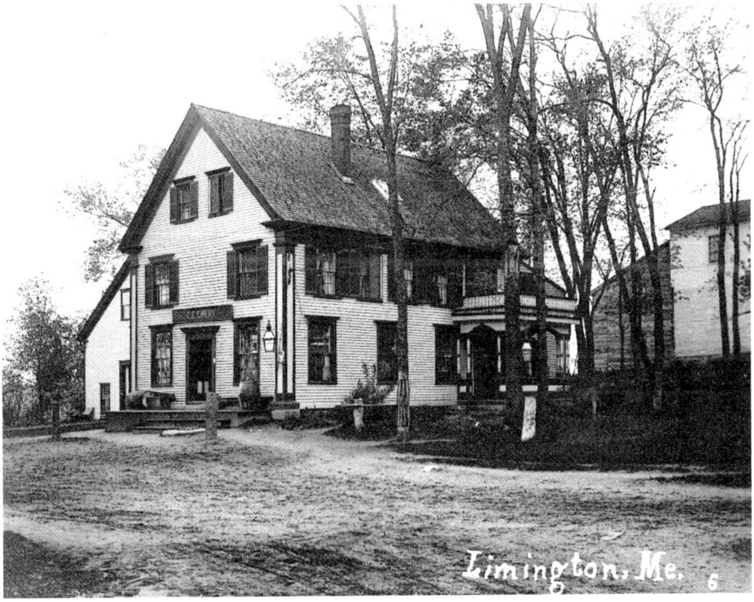

Limington Academy, in Limington, was incorporated in 1848 and its academy building was built in 1852. The dorm building shown here was originally a store and housed home economic classes on the first floor in the 1930s. The principal lived upstairs. It burned down in 1953. *Courtesy of Limington Historical Society.*

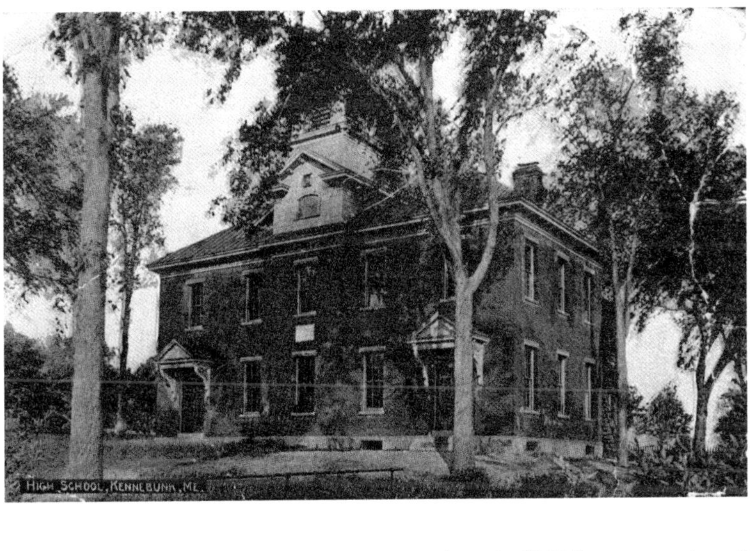

The Kennebunk High School, shown here, was torn down in 1921 for construction of a new school, later known as the Park Street School. It was built in 1870–71 after the Union Academy, which had stood on the site since 1833, burned down. The front section, shown here, was added in the 1890s. Park Street School was closed several years ago and the fate of the building has yet to be decided.

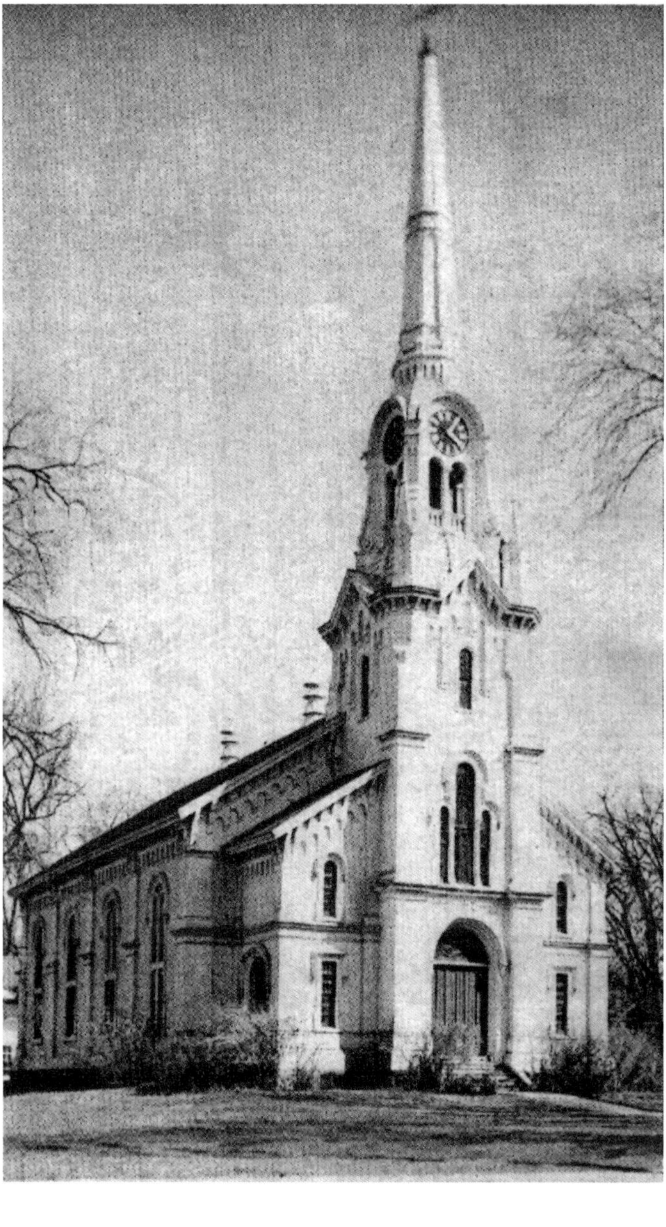

The First Congregational Church, built in 1863, stood on the corner of Main and Beech Streets in Saco. In 2000, it was destroyed by fire when a painter lit a cigarette near the steeple, which then ignited the fumes from the paint stripper being used and set the steeple ablaze.

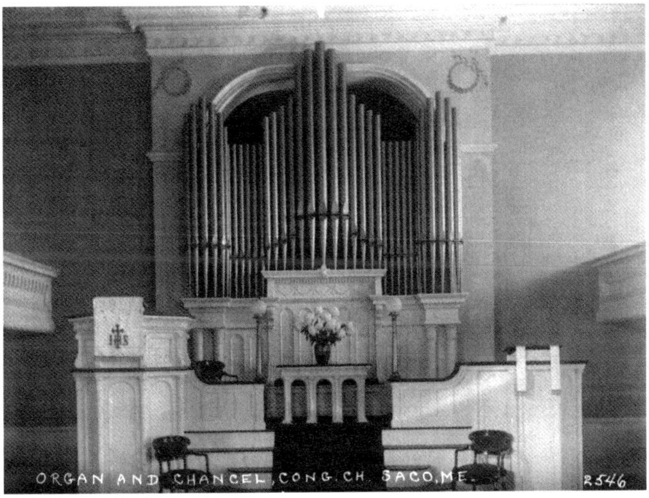

An interior view of the Saco Congregational Church showing the organ, which was lost when the church burned down. The church replaced an earlier one that had burned down on July 8, 1860. Boston architect John Calvin Stevens designed the new church in the Romanesque and Italianate style, with unique features such as the 126-foot spire, a four-faced clock and a recast Paul Revere bell that had been saved from the first church. It had beautiful stained-glass windows that were also destroyed. It's important to note that today there are many new paint strippers on the market that work really well and are nonflammable. Heat guns or blowtorches should never be used to remove paint from an old building.

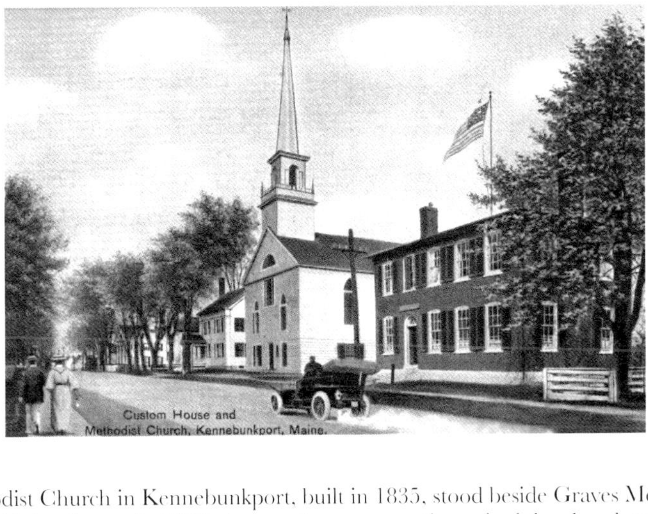

The Methodist Church in Kennebunkport, built in 1835, stood beside Graves Memorial Library on Maine Street. In 1862, the growing congregation raised the church up one story and added a lower floor. After 1900, membership began to dwindle, and in 1928 the steeple, added in 1882, was removed. The congregation disbanded and joined the Cape Porpoise Methodist Church in 1911. The American Legion used the building until 1960. It was then demolished for house lots.

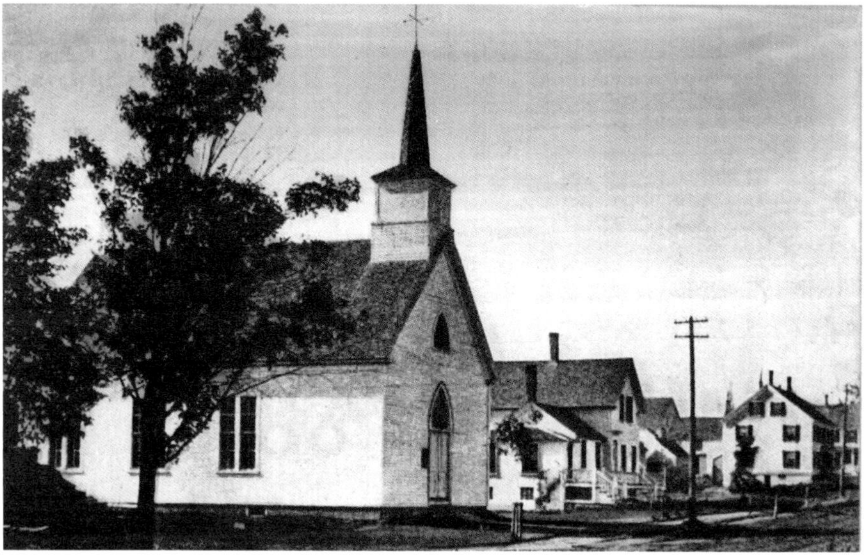

The Advent Church still stands in Berwick on Sullivan Street but has been converted to a garage. You can still tell it was a church and the steeple on top remains. The Advent Society began in 1880 and the church was built about 1890. It continued in use until about 1948, when the church disbanded. *Courtesy of Brian Cincotta.*

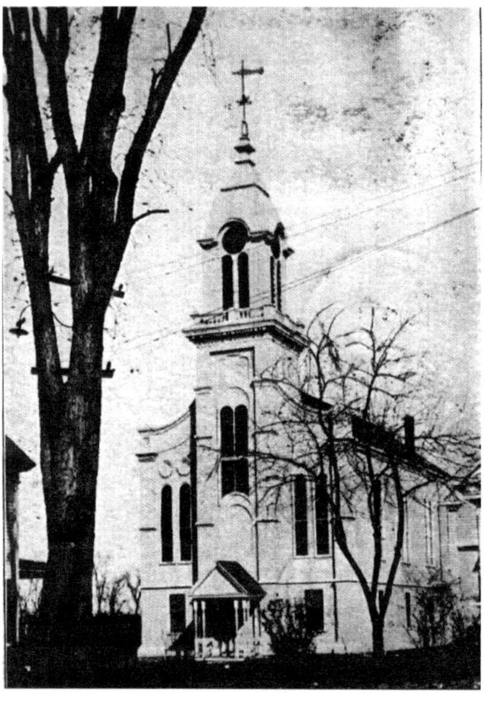

The First Baptist Church, originally located in South Berwick, was built in 1843. In 1866, the church was taken down and moved to Doughty Falls, now North Berwick. It was rebuilt in 1892 as it appears in this image, taken circa 1900, and burned down in 1906. Nine other Main Street buildings were also lost in the fire.

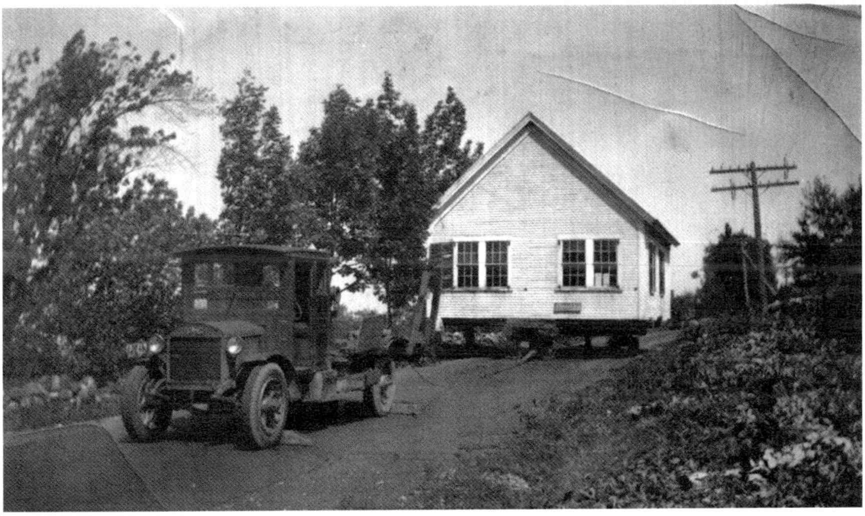

The Shaker school, in Alfred, was built in 1861 and is shown here as it was being moved to a new location in 1931. When the village was sold in 1931, the school was given to Alfred's American Legion Post and was moved to Route 202, where it still stands today, altered. *Courtesy of Friends of the Alfred Shakers Museum.*

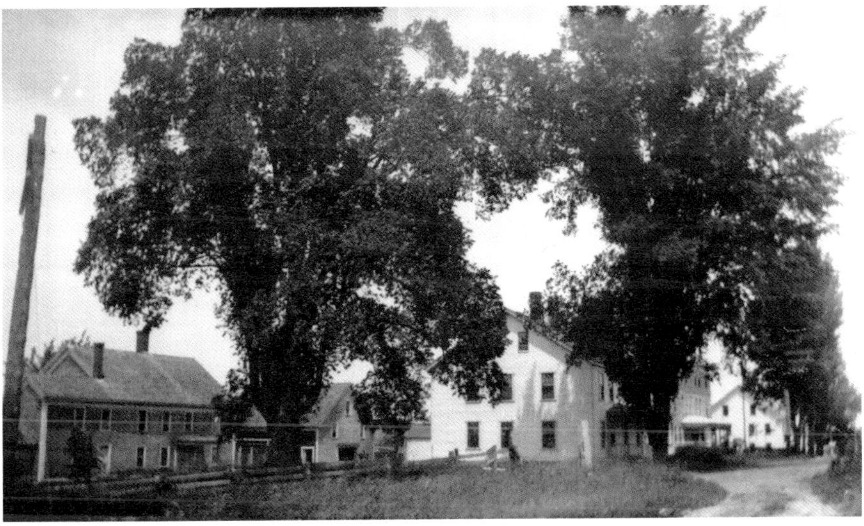

These Shaker buildings, in Alfred, were photographed before 1900. The building in the middle was the Girls' Shop and was built by Jabez Ricker, circa 1780. It was moved to Shaker Hill in 1796, where it still stands today, altered. Just beyond is the first dwelling house, which burned in 1901. To the left is the sisters' shop and laundry. *Courtesy of Friends of the Alfred Shakers Museum.*

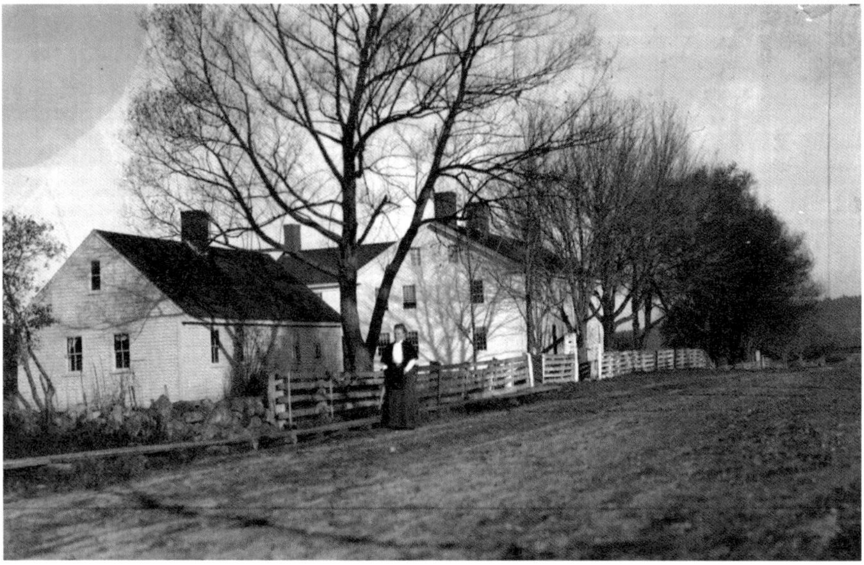

The second family dwelling house, circa 1900. The second family was established in 1800 and the dwelling house may have been built then. In 1919, it was sold to a Wells antique dealer, who salvaged hardware and woodwork and then demolished the building. The small building beside the dwelling house may have been the brethren's shop. *Courtesy of Friends of the Alfred Shakers Museum.*

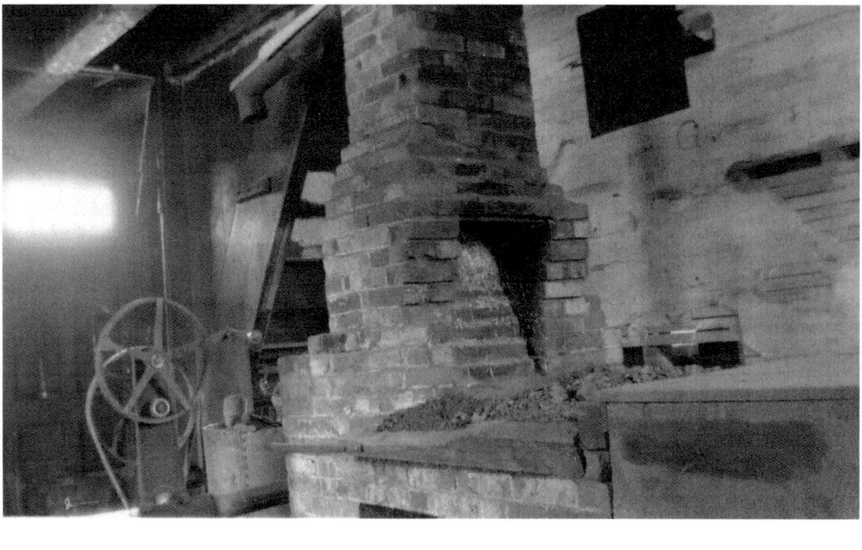

This is the interior of the blacksmith shop at the Shaker village. It was built in 1786 as the community's first meetinghouse. In 1794, it became a wheel shop. It was moved in 1878 and was made over as the new blacksmith shop after the old one was razed. It was moved in 1938 and could still be standing in the Alfred area. *Courtesy of Friends of the Alfred Shakers Museum.*

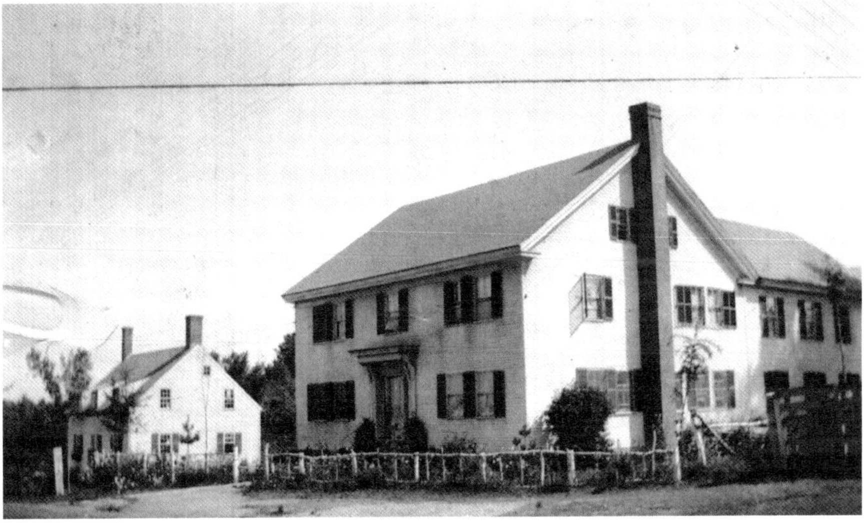

The trustee's house still stands but has been altered. Beyond it is the handyman's house, which was built before 1847 and no longer stands. *Courtesy of Friends of the Alfred Shakers Museum.*

CHAPTER SIX

Public Buildings and Town Views

This chapter contains images of town halls, train stations and town views that have changed over the last one hundred years or so. Town halls in various towns throughout the county have remarkable stories attached to them. Many of the smaller town halls were demolished when the towns outgrew them or they were used for other functions before being razed. In Wells, the third town hall was razed because it was too large, so a smaller one was built on the site. Several years later, the community had outgrown that town hall and had to build a bigger one at another site. In 1952, citizens of Kennebunkport decided they didn't need their town hall so they sold it. Thirty years later, they realized they needed a bigger town hall and bought back the old one, which had been converted to a Catholic church. The town debated the town hall problem for months, only to end up renovating the existing town hall and demolishing the Catholic church for a new fire station. York still has its old town hall and still uses it as town offices, and Kennebunk lost two to fire before the present building was built in 1921. The Berwicks together went through several town halls before ending up with the ones they have today. Eliot used the old Eliot High School for many years before demolishing it and building a new building. The early town halls were nothing more than large meeting halls that sometimes included a stage. Town officers usually worked from their homes or business places. Town business was minimal in those days, unlike today.

Train stations are another group of buildings that didn't last long. Although few burned, most were replaced or demolished as train lines were discontinued due to a decrease in ridership and loss of freight. Cars and trucks, along with the new Eisenhower Highway System, spelled the end of train service in the United States by the 1960s. Trolley lines began closing in the 1920s, to be replaced with buses. Some of the stations were moved and converted to other uses, like homes and cottages. Others became restaurants and shops. Some just disappeared. South Berwick's station was moved to Wells in the early 1990s and dumped in a field, where it has been left sitting and rotting all this time. Now that train service has been restored to York County, new stations are being built to accommodate riders traveling between Boston and Portland.

Town views are another ever-changing facet as old buildings come down and new developments are built, forever altering the landscape. One of the huge losses for many towns has been the elm trees that once lined New England streets for over one hundred years. They succumbed to the Dutch elm disease in the 1970s and 1980s and had to be cut down. Rebuilt bridges, straightened roads and new construction, along with the loss of older homes and buildings, have altered the landscape of York County.

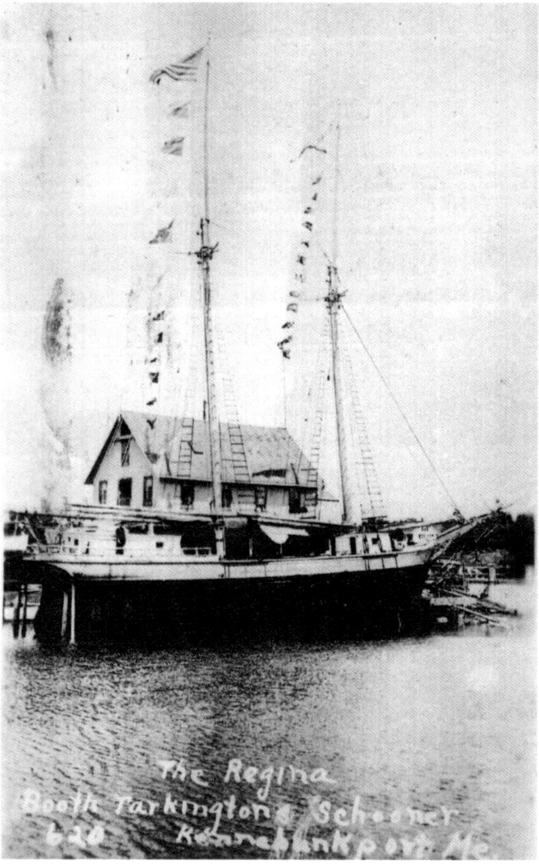

Writer Booth Tarkington summered in Kennebunkport and owned a large summer home there, now converted to condominiums. Originally from Indiana, he used this boat, the *Regina*, as a writing studio, and it was a popular landmark along Ocean Avenue for many years. Tarkington died in 1946 and in 1952 the ship was towed out to sea and sunk.

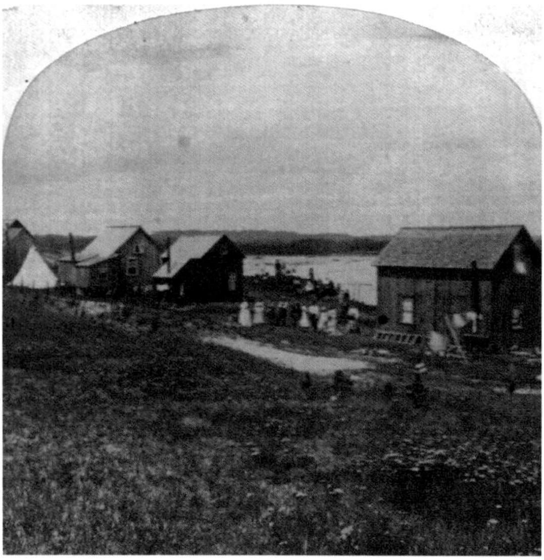

Concordville, York Beach, was on the peninsula where Nubble Light and Sohier Park are located. It was an area named for the large number of people from Concord, New Hampshire, who camped and summered there. These primitive camps no longer exist.

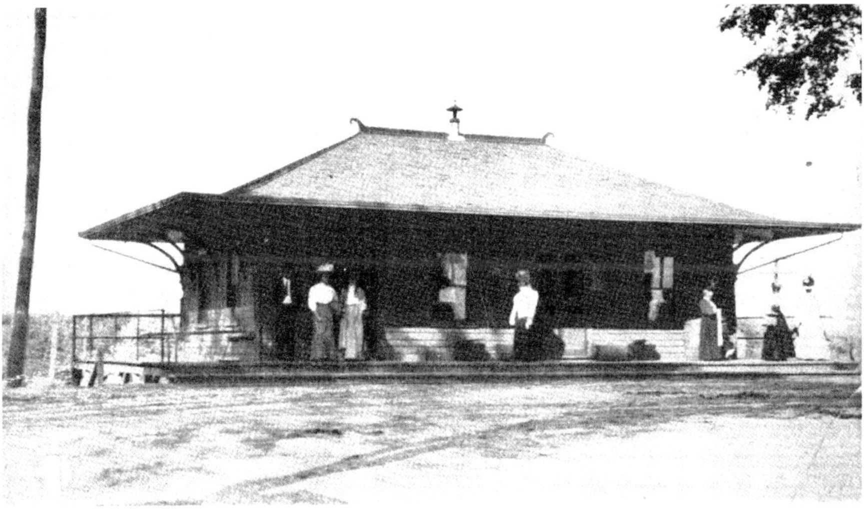

The Kennebunk "Electric Railway" station was located on Depot Street near the B&M train station. Several private trolley lines merged with the Atlantic Shore Line Railway in 1904, becoming one of the largest intercity trolley systems in the state of Maine. The Atlantic Shore Line provided service to the entire southern Maine seacoast and several inland towns as well.

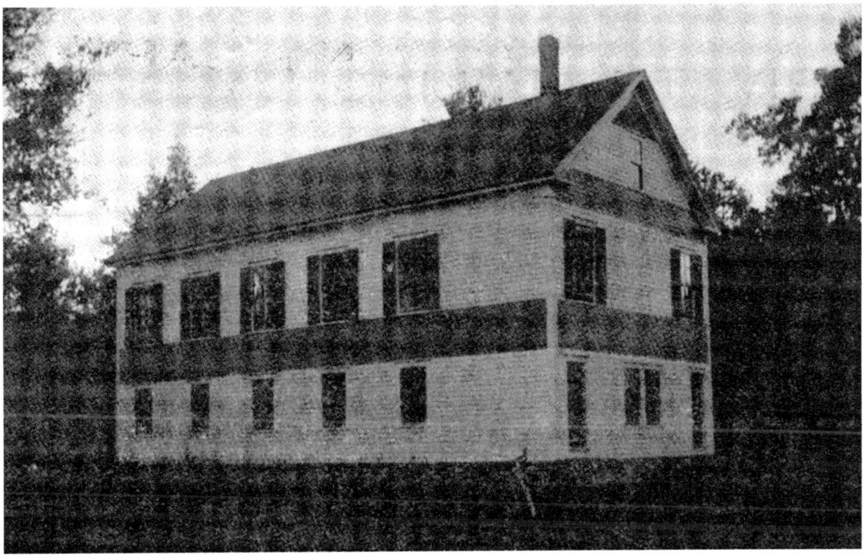

The Bauneg Beg Grange, shortly after its construction in 1902. It was located on the western shore of Bauneg Beg Lake, in North Berwick. It burned down in 1923 and was replaced.

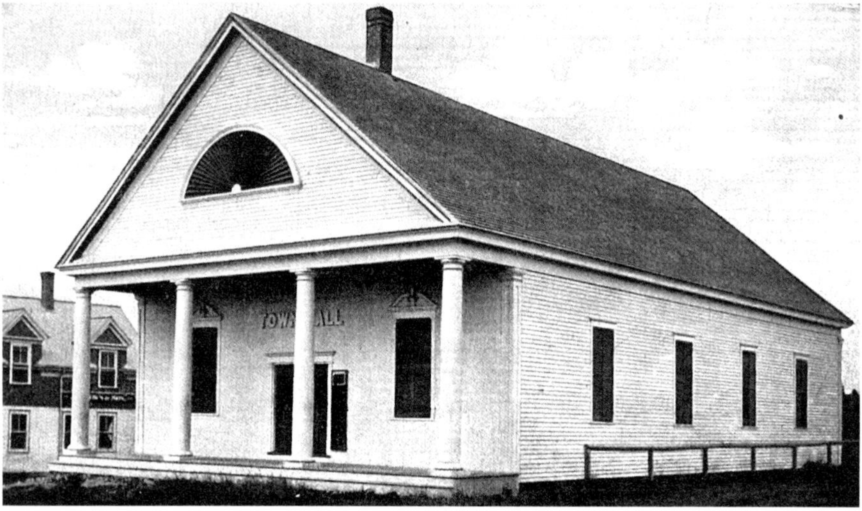

One of the characteristics attributed to the New England Yankee is thrift, or "Waste Not Want Not." That's certainly true when it comes to the old Kennebunkport Town Hall, shown here. It originally stood next to the town's poor farm, on Arundel Road. It was built in 1902 and replaced an earlier town hall that had been outgrown. At the time, the location was central and also on the trolley line, which made it easy for town residents to get there. In 1916, the northern part of the town became North Kennebunkport (today known as Arundel) and Arundel Road became the dividing line between the two towns. That placed the poor farm and the town hall in Arundel, but it was agreed that they would remain part of Kennebunkport unless they became private property. By 1952, it was decided that the town no longer needed the town hall and it was sold to the Arundel Opera Theatre. It dismantled the building and moved it to North Street, where it was rebuilt, reusing almost all of the original building. Its third incarnation began in 1964 when the theatre was sold to St. Martha's Church, which rebuilt it again, transforming it into a new Catholic church. It might have had another life after the church was closed and the congregation merged with the Catholic church in Kennebunk, but it wasn't to be. Because of all the rebuilding, which occurred before the current building codes were enacted, the building was found to have structural problems that made it impossible to convert it back into a town hall for Kennebunkport. The building was demolished and a new fire station was built on the land. *Courtesy of Greg Hubbard.*

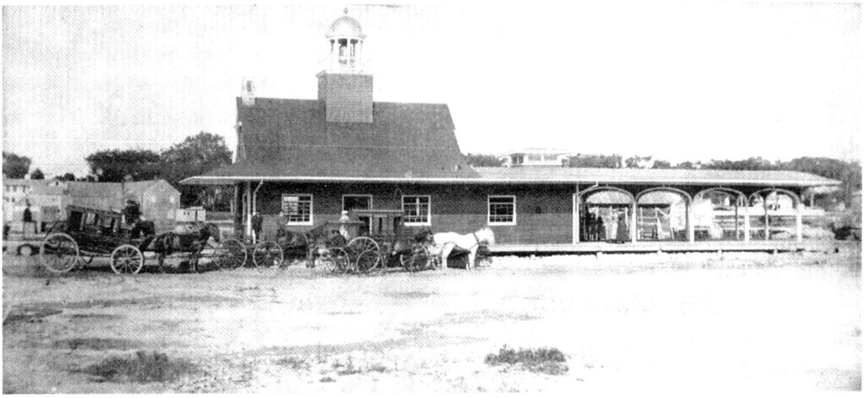

The Kennebunkport station, circa 1890, as it looked after completion in 1883. The line connected the Kennebunk depot with Kennebunkport. The opening of the line spurred a building boom in Kennebunkport and Kennebunk Beach and made it easier for tourists to get to the resort hotels. The line was discontinued in the late 1920s and part of the station still survives and is used as a restaurant today. *Courtesy of Greg Hubbard.*

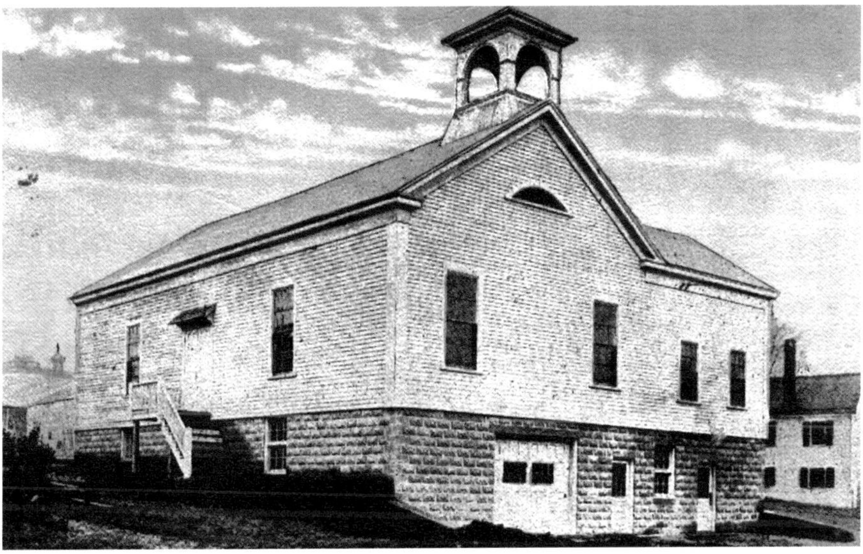

The old Berwick Town Hall stood where Berwick's fire station is located today. After the new town hall was built, the American Legion occupied this building. *Courtesy of Brian Cincotta.*

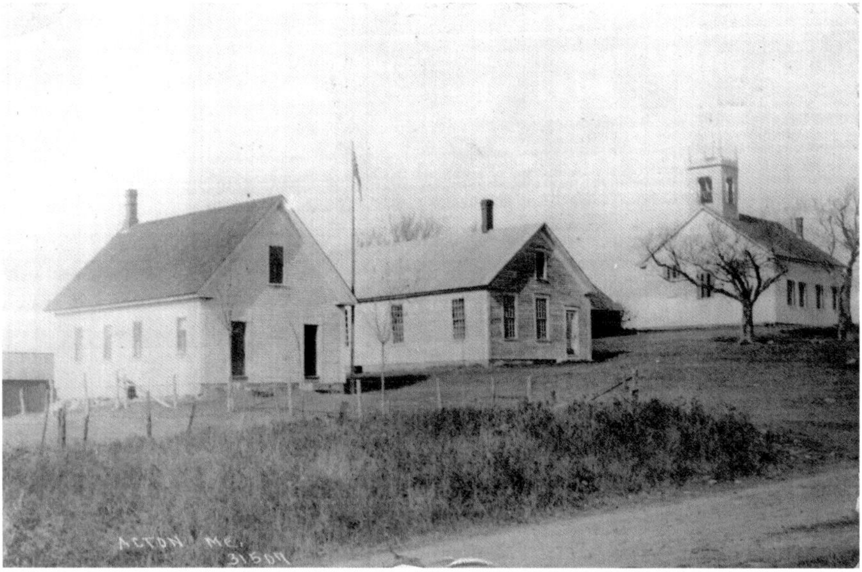

Acton Corner, Acton, circa 1915. The school, on the left, was built in 1886 and closed in 1937. In 1957, the town library moved there. The town hall in the middle is also gone. The Acton Corner Church, on the right, still stands.

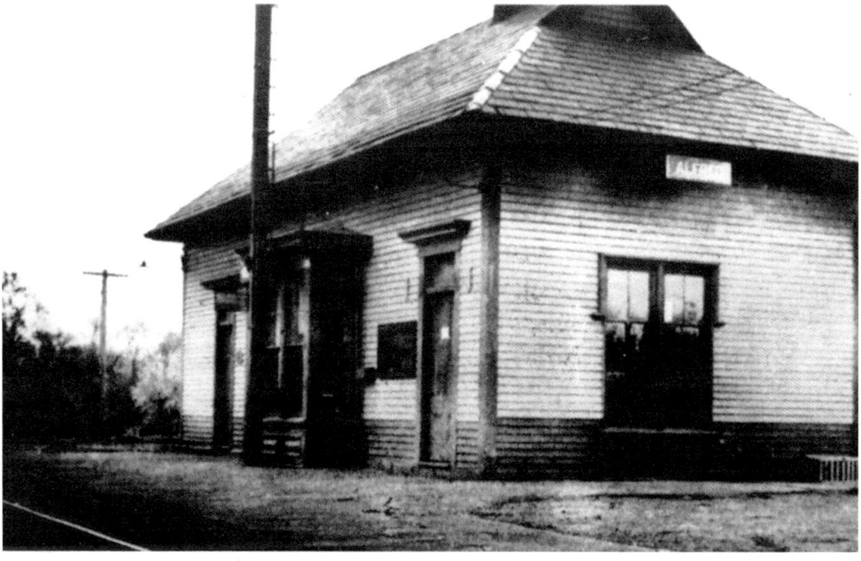

The Alfred Train Station, in Alfred, no longer stands.

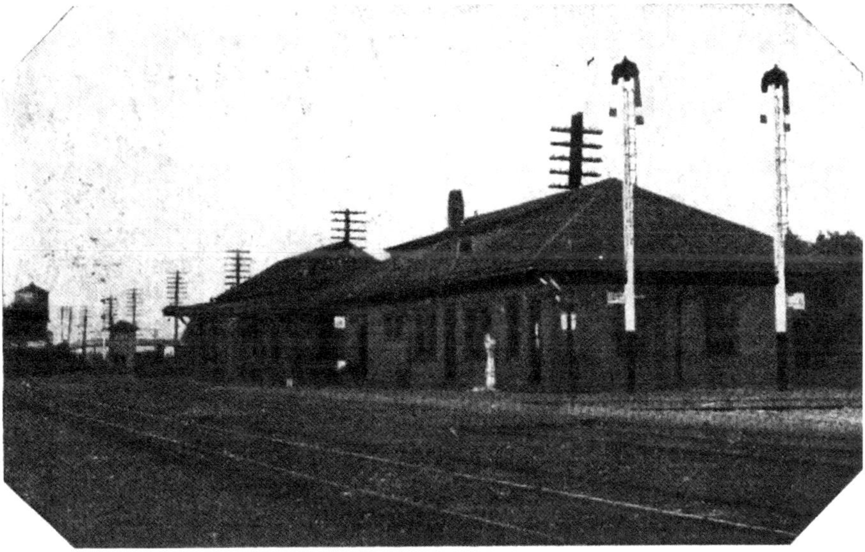

North Berwick train stations. The station in back is the old one and no longer stands. The new station in front was built in 1907 and still stands today and is used as a trucking terminal. The last train left the station on August 30, 1952.

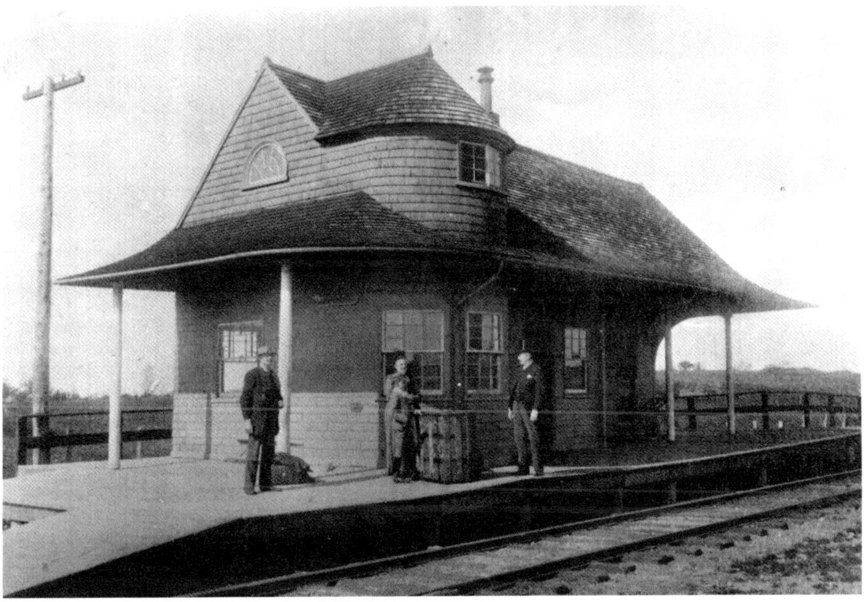

The Kennebunk Beach station was built in 1883 when the line from the Kennebunk train station to Kennebunkport opened. After the line closed in 1926, it was moved to Great Hill Road and was converted to a cottage.

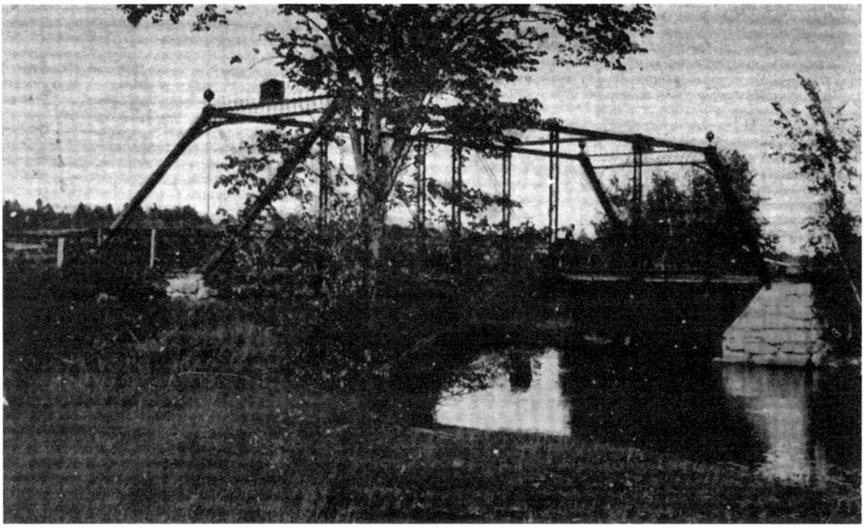

Eddy's Bridge, in Berwick, on the Salmon Falls River, was replaced in 1968.

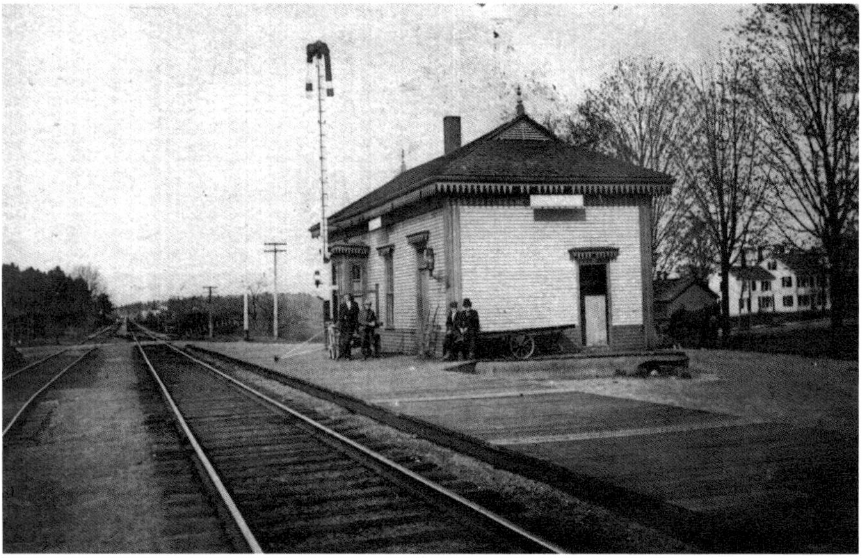

Bar Mills station was located on Depot Road and no longer stands. *Courtesy of Buxton-Hollis Historical Society.*

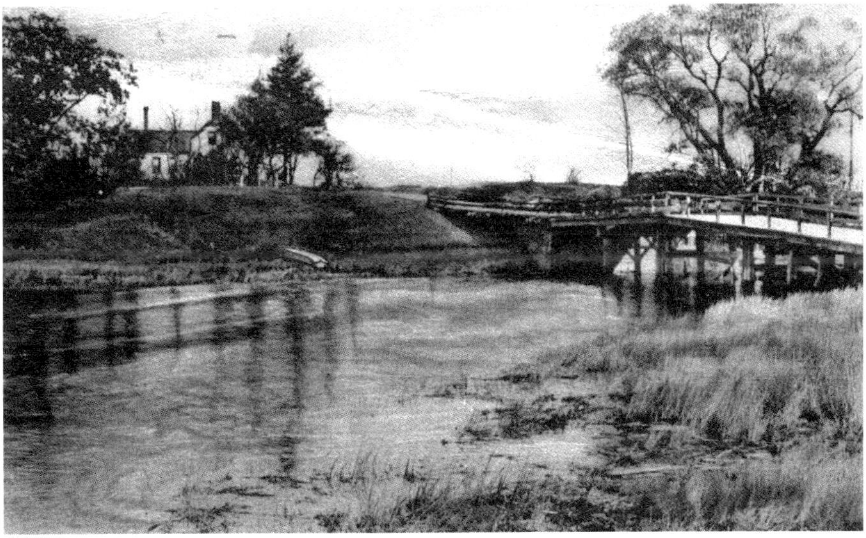

Durrell's drawbridge, over the Kennebunk River in Kennebunk, circa 1900. The drawbridge allowed ships built at the landing to pass through on their way to Kennebunkport. Today this is Durrell's Bridge Road and the home on the left is the Durrell family home, now gone.

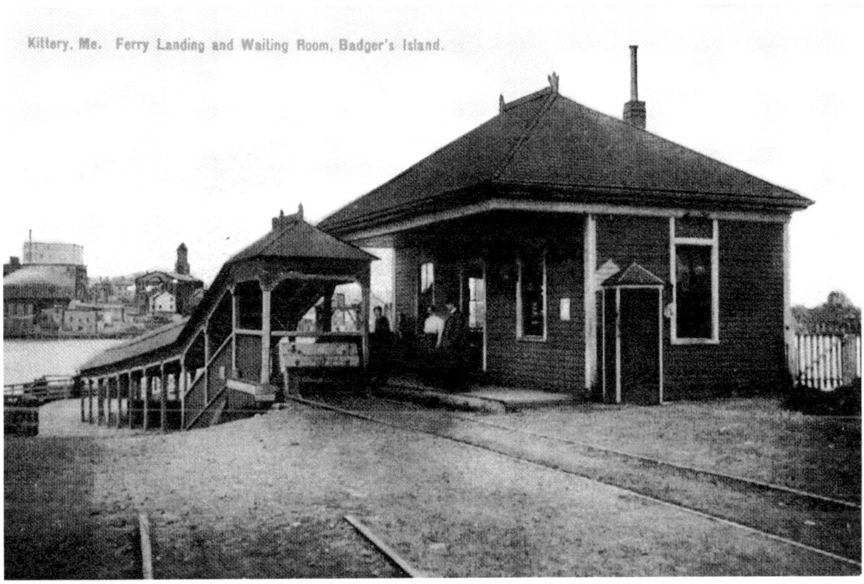

The Ferry Landing and waiting room on Badger's Island in Kittery, early 1900s. *Courtesy of Newfield Historical Society.*

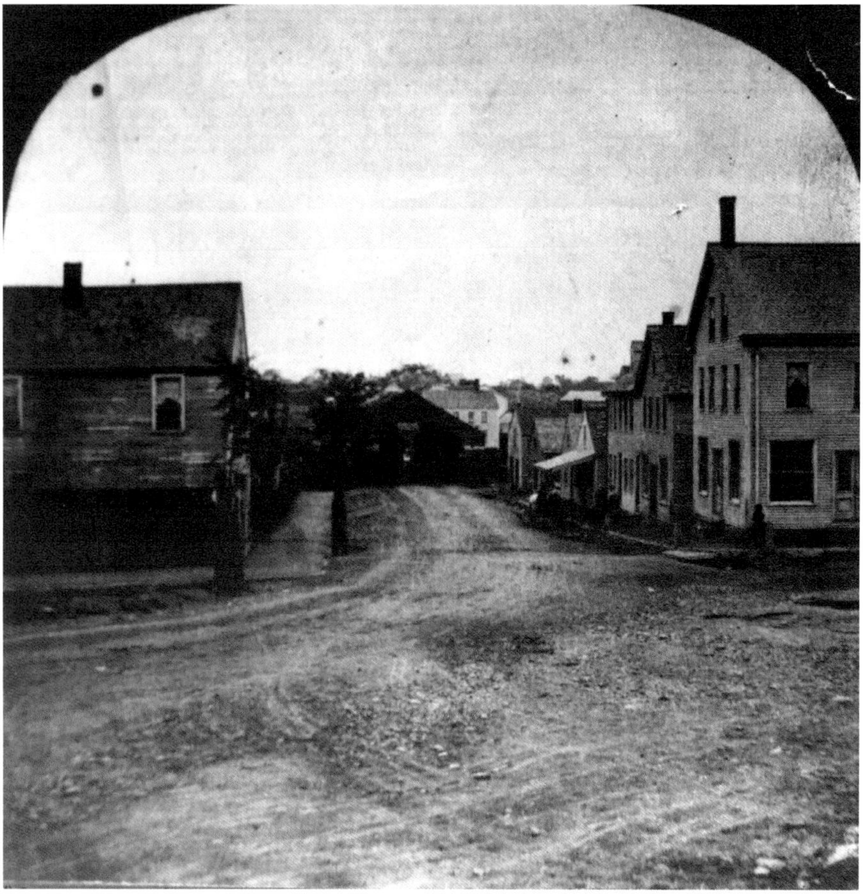

The covered bridge over the Saco River connected Biddeford to Factory Island and Saco. It was replaced in 1877 with the iron bridge seen on page 122. All of the buildings seen here are gone. *Courtesy of McArthur Library*.

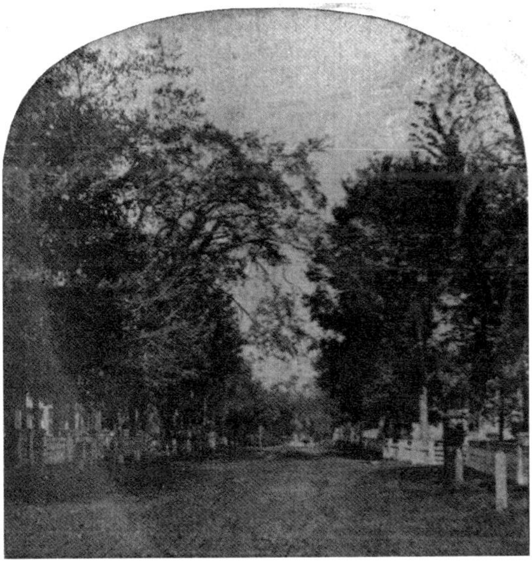

The elm trees that once lined the villages of York County towns, and all of New England, provided shade for over one hundred years. They are indelibly etched in people's minds but only exist now in period films and photographs. Dutch elm disease devastated elm trees throughout New England and they had to be cut down.

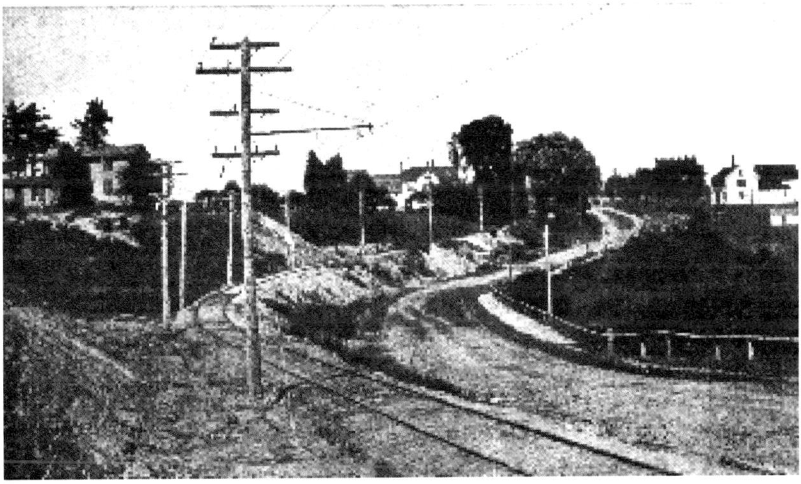

Virtually unrecognizable today is the historic Buffum Hill area of Wells, shown in this early postcard. This is Route 1 before it was straightened, and the trolley tracks date the picture to circa 1920. Buffum Hill was the site of an early settlement and for many years a sawmill operated here. In the eighteenth century, a garrison was located here to protect settlers from Indian attacks. The house on the right is gone, and the house on the left has been mutilated beyond recognition. The house in the middle still stands and is a motel today. *Courtesy of Wells-Ogunquit Historical Society.*

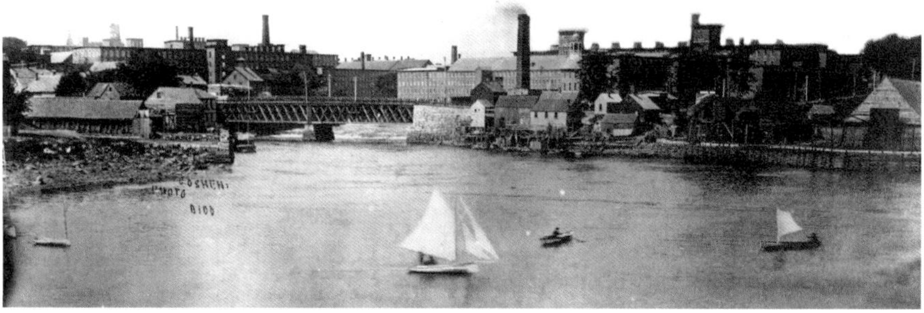

Looking up the Saco River, Biddeford is on the left and Factory Island is on the right. All of the buildings along the riverbanks are long gone. Factory Island was once known as Indian Island and Cutt's Island and was once owned by Elisha Ayers, who moved to Newfield in 1790 and helped found that town. *Courtesy of McArthur Library.*

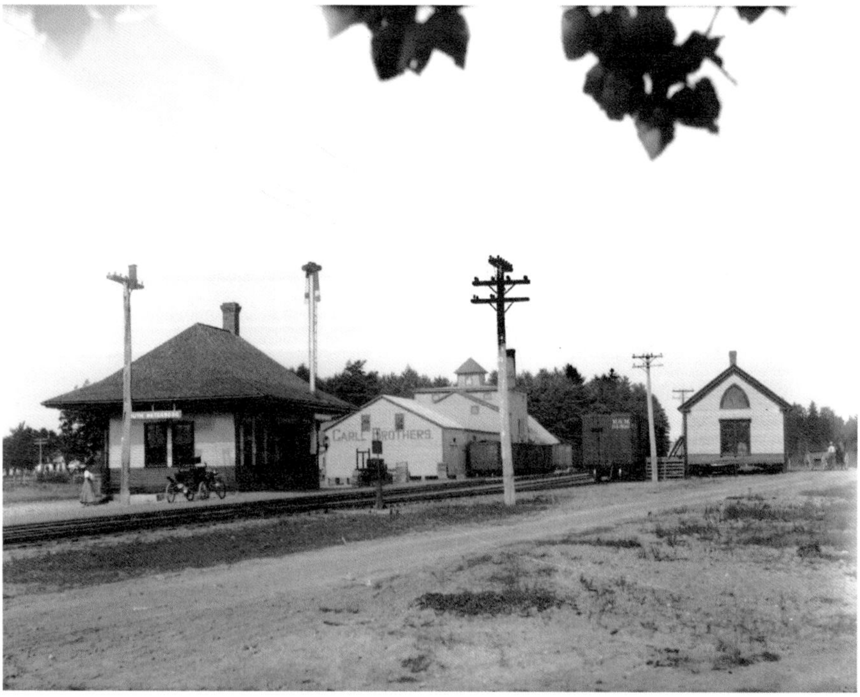

The Waterboro station, location unknown. *Courtesy of Sanford-Springfield Historical Society.*

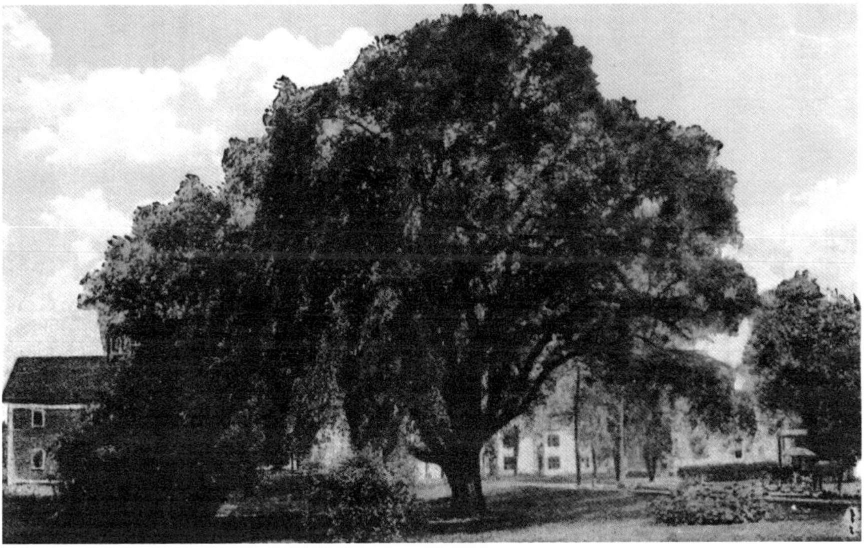

The Lafayette Elm, in Kennebunk, was planted to commemorate General Lafayette's 1825 visit to Kennebunk. It was the second largest elm in the state and was 131 feet tall with a girth of 17 feet, 3 inches. It succumbed to Dutch elm disease and was taken down in the early 1970s.

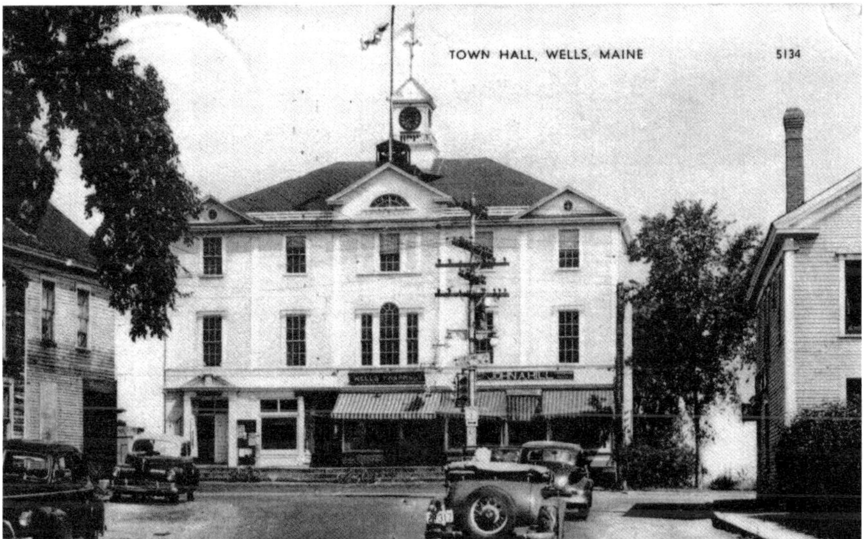

The third Wells Town Hall stood where the Wells Fire Department is located today. It was built in 1912 after the second town hall burned down. It seems that part of the burned town hall was incorporated into the new building, as there are many similarities between the two buildings. The third town hall was razed in 1967, but the clock tower was saved, and a few years ago it was placed on the roof of a Kennebunk barn, where it has been left to rot.

Bibliography

Albert, J. Wilfrid, ed., et al. *The Story of Berwick.* Somersworth, NH: New Hampshire Publishing Company, 1963.

Alfred Courthouse, deeds and probate.

Alley, Margo. *Biddeford Pool: A Founding History*. N.p.: Instant Publisher, 2006.

Ayers, Ruth Bridges. *Early Families of Newfield, Maine*. N.p.: Penobscot Press, 1995.

Bardwell, John D. *Ogunquit by the Sea.* Augusta, ME: Alan Sutton Publishing, Inc., 1994.

———. *Old York Beach.* Augusta, ME: Alan Sutton Publishing, Inc., 1994.

———. *Old York Beach Volume II*. Dover, NH: Arcadia Publishing, 1996.

Biddeford Journal

Blanney, Daniel E. *Old Orchard Beach*. Charleston, SC: Arcadia Publishing, 2007.

Burr, Steven. *Kennebunk Main Street.* Dover, NH: Arcadia Publishing, 1995.

———. *The Kennebunks in Season*. Charleston, SC: Arcadia Publishing, 2005.

Burrage, Henry S., Rev. "Colonel Nathaniel Sparhawk of Kittery." *Collections of the Maine Historical Society* 9. Portland, ME: Thurston Print, 1898.

Butler,.Joyce. *A Kennebunkport Album*. Portland, ME: Portland Lithograph Co., 1984.

———. *Kennebunkport Scrapbook, Vol. 1*. N.p.: Thomas Murphy, Publisher, 1977.

———. *Wildfire Loose: The Week Maine Burned*. Kennebunkport, ME: Durrell Publications, n.d.

Domingue, Robert A. *Greetings from Old Orchard Maine: A Picture Postcard History*. Wilmington, MA: Hampshire Press, 1986.

Donahue, Marie. *The Old Academy on the Hill*. Camden, ME: Picton Press, 1992.

Downs, Jacques. *The Cities on the Saco*. Norfolk, VA: Donning Company/ Publishers, 1985.

Duncan, Charlotte. "Whistling Oyster: The True Story of a Successful Teahouse." *The House Beautiful* (August 1916).

Dutch, Davis E., and Janet Robie Hooke, eds. *Doughty Falls*. Portsmouth, NH: Peter E. Randall Publisher, LLC, 2006.

Eastman, Harland H. *Alfred, Maine: The Shakers and the Village*. Sanford, ME: Wilson's Printers, n.d.

———. *A Cluster of Maine Villages: Sanford and Springvale and Alfred*. Sanford, ME: Wilson's Printers, 1991.

———. *Sanford and Springvale, Maine—A Backward Glance*. Sanford, ME: Wilson's Printers, 1988.

———. *Sanford and Springvale, Maine—In the Days of Fred Philpot*. Second Edition. Sanford, ME: Wilson's Printers, 1993.

———. *Villages on the Mousam: Sanford and Springvale, Maine*. Sanford, ME: Wilson's Printers, 1995.

Emery, Edwin. *History of Sanford, Maine*. Sanford, ME: Harlan H. Eastman, 1987.

Frost, John Eldridge. *Colonial Village*. Kittery Point, ME: Gundlow Club, Inc., n.d. Second printing Milford, NH: Cabinet Press, Inc., 1980.

Harkness, Seth. "Last days of a Route 1 icon." *Portland Press Herald Maine Sunday Telegram*, March 7, 2008.

Joy, Kenneth. *The Kennebunks "Out of the Past."* Freeport, ME: Bond Wheelwright Company, 1967.

Kittery, Ancient and Modern Kittery—The Gateway to Maine, the Oldest Incorporated Township in the State. Kittery Booklet Committee, 1931.

Libby, Steve, ed. *Newfield Maine…the First 200 Years*. Town of Newfield, Maine, 1976.

Magnuson, Rosalind. *Trunks, Textiles & Transits: Manufacturing on the Mousam River*. Kennebunk, ME: Brick Store Museum, 2005.

New York Times. "Fire Merely Hastens Old Orchard's Doom: Its Decline Began Ten Years Ago with Advent of Trolley Cars and Cheap Excursion Trains," August 18, 1907.

The Ossipee Valley. Charleston, SC: Arcadia Publishing, 2005.

Perkins, Esselyn Gilman. *History of Ogunquit Village*. Portland, ME: Falmouth Publishing House, 1951.

Pirsig, Wendy. *The Placenames of South Berwick*. Portsmouth, NH: Black Channel Press, 2007.

Portland Press Herald

Remich, Daniel. *History of Kennebunk.* N.p.: 1911.

Robinson, J. Dennis. *Strawbery Banke: A Seaport Museum 400 Years in the Making.* Portsmouth, NH: Peter E. Randall Publisher, LLC, 2007.

Scully, Jeffery A. *Saco.* Augusta, ME: Alan Sutton Publishing, Inc., 1994.

Seaman, Charles Littlefield, and Dorothy A. Seaman. *A Pictorial History of Ogunquit.* Sanford, ME: Wilson's Printers, 1993.

Shelley, Hope M. *My Name Is Wells I Am the Town.* N.p.: Penobscot Press, 2002.

Sleeper, Frank H. *Buxton, Hollis, and Limington.* Dover, NH: Arcadia Publishing, 1997.

Spiller, Virginia S., ed. *350 Years as York.* Copyright 2001 by the Town of York 350th Anniversary Committee.

Taylor, Robert. *History of Limington, Maine 1668–1900.* N.p.: Oxford Hills Press, 1975.

Treadwell, Olive M., et al. *Sesquicentennial History of Acton, Maine 1830–1980.* N.p.: n.d.

Whitaker, Jan. *Tea at the Blue Lantern Inn: A Social History of the Tea Room Craze in America.* New York: St. Martin's Press, 2002.

About the Author

Steven Burr, a Maine native born in Kennebunk, has enjoyed a lifelong interest in local history. He has researched and written about local history and events for more than twenty years, specializing in work related to historic preservation. He was the historian at First Parish Church, Kennebunk's oldest church, for ten years and has volunteered for local libraries and museums. This is his third book.